W9-BRJ-721

doing
good
by
doing
little

doing good by doing little

Race and Schooling in Britain

David L. Kirp

University of California Press
Berkeley, Los Angeles, London

University of California Press
Berkeley and Los Angeles, California
University of California Press, Ltd.
London, England

ISBN 0-520-03740-5
Library of Congress Catalog Card Number: 78-62824
Printed in the United States of America

1 2 3 4 5 6 7 8 9

to D. W. V.

Contents

Preface

Assessments of race policy are tricky business, particularly when undertaken by an outsider to the nation whose policies are being assessed. My own experiences in Israel, the Netherlands, as well as in Britain, while undertaking this analysis, indicate the existence of a widespread belief that racial issues are both wholly idiosyncratic and hence not susceptible of any comparative treatment, and so much a part of the fabric of the nation that one not a member of the society could not hope to make sense of them.

There is enough truth in both beliefs to warrant caution. A great deal of race policy is idiosyncratic—attributable, for example, to the circumstances under which the nonwhite population arrived in the country, the country's historical relationships with nonwhites, and traditions of public and private problem solving (including the extent to which formal rather than informal problem-solving mechanisms are relied upon). Even things which on the surface appear comparable sometimes turn out to be very different: for example, one who equates "busing" in the United States, Britain, and Israel does so at considerable peril. And race policy needs to be appreciated not as an isolatable experience but rather at least partly as deriving from broad social and political context. One needs to know about a great deal that is not explicitly linked to race in order to make sense of race policy.

Studies published by international organizations often finesse these concerns by aiming their analyses at such a remove from concrete circumstance that it becomes hard at times to remember that real nations and real people are the subject of discussion. This book takes a very different and altogether riskier approach. It is rooted in the particular, not just of race and schooling in Britain but also of other aspects of the story—among them, the decline of Empire, the nature of universalist social policy, and the evolution of state schooling reform—that bear on race. It takes the perspective of a sympathetic outsider whose struggles to make sense of what he perceives are recorded on every page. That outsider status has all the readily apparent pitfalls; it also brings with it certain advantages, among them the capacity to disentangle the unique from the commensurate and a usefully unfamiliar perspective towards a history that the British tend to take for granted.

If the inquiry has enabled me to learn something about Britain, it has clarified my understanding of American race policy as well. I have come to appreciate, for instance, just how extraordinary is the American reliance on the judiciary as an institution for addressing problems in this realm, and more generally how the conversion of social issues into legal issues affects their resolution; I have also grown to appreciate how a given policy instrument such as busing acquires very different meanings in different contexts. In some ways, I crossed the Atlantic in order to understand America better. That new understanding too is reported here.

This book is not a comparative study in the traditional sense, for I wanted to say more about the emphatically British view of race and schooling than a comparative framework would have permitted. Considerable discussion of American policy is nonetheless interwoven into the text, in order to offer clarity through comparison. The inquiry is meant to address the continuing policy debates over race in both Britain and the United States. If it succeeds at that task, it does so not by offering up answers—only a naif or a savant would attempt answers in a realm so multifaceted and murky as race policy—but by clarifying and sharpening the terms of the debate.

For a slim volume, my debts are numerous. A Travelling Fellowship from the Ford Foundation enabled me to spend four months in England conducting interviews and collecting primary source material. A Spencer Fellowship, awarded by the National Academy of Education, gave me the luxury of time to turn a rough outline into a finished book. The Institute for United States Studies, University of London, and the Van Leer Jerusalem Foundation provided the space and the intellectual yeast for me to complete a first draft. Further work was done at my home institution, the Graduate School of Public Policy, University of California (Berkeley), a place of exceptional collegiality and civility.

Personal debts are equally substantial. Fred Wirt sparked my interest in British race policy with his pioneering work in the field. Dozens of people in Britain, both in and out of the academy, helped steer me clear of the predictable sins an outsider might commit. Especially helpful were Maurice Kogan, A. H. Halsey, Brian Holmes, Stewart Maclure, John Lyttle, Anthony Lester, and Allan Little. Gail Saliterman assisted me in the early stages of research and in undertaking early interviews; Michael Doying tracked down countless stray references. My colleagues Martin Trow, Mark Yudof, David Tyack, Thomas Laqueur, Nathan Glazer, Sheldon Rothblatt, Paul Mishkin, and Richard de Neufville each gave the manuscript a careful critical reading. To all of them my especial thanks.

one

A British Dilemma: Public Policy, Private Policy, and Race

Inexplicitness as a Policy Preference

With as little fuss as possible, Britain has gone about the business of providing an education for its ever-growing number of nonwhite children. What that group, now some 4 percent of the primary and secondary school population, receives differs as little as possible from what is generally available. Those educational distinctions that are drawn are not color-based. There is special language instruction, for example, to aid those—largely immigrants from India, Bangladesh, and Pakistan—for whom English is a second language. Additional money is channelled by the national government to local educational authorities[1] "required . . . to incur expenditure by reason . . . of special social need"—a category taken to include nonwhites.

Even these policies appear concessions to the inevitable, not the preferred approach; the distinctions they make are kept as blurred as possible. And they also constitute the special policy case. At present, there exist no educational programs aimed directly at nonwhites, no deliberate efforts to school nonwhites and whites together, and little concern with the possibility of racial discrimination in education. At least as a matter of official educational policy, the British minimize the relevance of color. The same point may be made about British social policy generally. Whether with respect to health, welfare, employment, or housing, Britain has self-consciously diminished the significance of race.[2] Race plays only an inexplicit part in the policy-making calculus.

As deployed here, inexplicitness is meant to convey two distinct meanings. In the usual instance, inexplicitness implies doing nothing concerning race. The term also may mean doing good by stealth. A decent proportion of the "special social need" aid, for instance, goes to authorities with large numbers of nonwhite students. In this instance, race is tacitly understood, but not mandated, to be such a "social need." Race may be a predicate for positive policy, as long—and, as other policy illustrations will make clear, only as long—as no one takes official notice of the fact.

The first three chapters of this book undertake to report and analyze the working of racial inexplicitness. Chapter One looks to the policy's historic origins, in shared private attitudes and in official efforts, and sketches the operation of the policy in the sphere of race relations generally. Chapter Two hones in on schooling, inquiring into the evolution of the policy of inexplicitness; it reviews debates over the desirability of special aid programs, programs aimed at assimilation, racial headcounting, and the like to illumine the governmental preference for not confronting racial issues as such. The third chapter focuses on one clearly racial policy adopted with respect to schooling: the busing, or dispersal, of nonwhites. Busing, unlike any of the other policies canvassed, is explicitly racial. It is, however, just this fact that constituted the chief cause of its demise, and in that sense the experience serves as the apparent exception that proves the rule.

The British do not speak of "inexplicit" policy considerations. No matter: the practice so clearly accords with generally held views concerning the role of government in this sphere that its rightness is seldom questioned. Racial inexplicitness does not embody an inevitability; it is, rather, a deliberate policy choice.

This point is most clearly established by contrasting the British approach with that taken by the United States, where race as such has been very much an item on the policy agenda for at least the past quarter-century, since the Supreme Court in *Brown v. Board of Education*[3] held unconstitutional the maintenance of racially "separate but equal" schools. All three branches of government have been busy defining the meaning of nondiscrimination with respect to race. The questions addressed are exquisitely difficult: Are only explicit racial distinctions offensive, or are seemingly neutral practices which operate to disadvantage blacks equally impermissible? Is the reason or motive underlying a racial differentiation relevant, or should policy attention be focused exclusively on the racial effect of the practice? Should the goal of social policy in the racial domain be equality of opportunity irrespective of race, or rather equality of result?[4] These questions concerning racial nondiscrimination merge into a second, related set of puzzles concerning the permissibility of government's taking race into account in order to aid, not disadvantage, racial minorities; the problem is more succinctly framed in terms of "preferential treatment" or "reverse discrimination."[5]

The last chapter draws on the British experience and the counterpart American history in appraising the policy of inexplicitness. The histories of the two countries with respect to race differ greatly, but comparisons between them are still useful, for they can shed light on ignored points of commensurability. Moreover, although inexplicitness is consistent with a host of British social policy considerations extrinsic to race—a preference for consensually made decisions, for instance—as the first three chapters establish, the British approach embodies a deliberate policy response to the nonwhite presence, one which necessarily rejects the explicit, or American, alternative. That fact too makes comparisons intriguing.

Does inexplicitness work? In the realm of race relations, in which no policy choice seems especially satisfying, evaluating inexplicitness involves not a selection of the best but a determination of the least bad. That task is studded with pitfalls. One's preference will be partly premised on normative considerations: What relationship between government and the governed is preferred? What should be the relevance for policy of status differences? That preference will also be partly rooted in empirically based assessments of what has apparently succeeded, at least in a particular time and place (a process confounded, to be sure, by disagreements concerning the measure and causes of success). The concluding chapter frames these issues with the intention of encouraging intelligent—and explicit—policy debates over the merits of racial inexplicitness, both in Britain and the United States.

Questions concerning the efficacy of inexplicitness as a policy choice need to be postponed, pending a recounting of the policy's evolution. That history properly begins with the reaction of the British to the influx of nonwhites in the 1950s and early 1960s, as embodied both in initial governmental responses and the behavior of ordinary citizens.

Strange and New

Ultimately, the determining element
in deciding the future of race relations
in Britain is the character of British

> society and the manner in which it
> responds to the stresses set up during
> the process of adaptation and change.[6]

> If only we British, who are so fond of
> travelling in the body, would also
> travel a little in the soul![7]

The End of Empire. The beginning of substantial immigration of nonwhites[8] to Britain almost precisely coincides with the nation's decision to extricate itself from the Empire. Uniquely among colonial nations, Britain had made its subjects citizens both of colony and mother country. While that relationship was in good part formalistic, "a lawyer's attempt to give substance to the fading shadow of the imperial connection,"[9] the maintenance of dual citizenship even as one-time colonies became independent states signalled Britain's recognition of a continuing obligation to the inhabitants of territory long ruled by her.[10] Had this sense of obligation not been present, it is unlikely that Britain would ever have witnessed a substantial nonwhite immigration.

The end of Empire also profoundly affected the reception that Britain accorded to the new immigrants, at both the official and unofficial, the public and private levels. The public level is the more obvious and readily treated: public policy, the response of government to the dilemmas presented by immigration, was influenced by the perceived lessons of the colonialist era.

The reactions of individual Britons were also, if more nebulously, colored by the need to cope with what was thought to be a change in the very character of the nation. These personal reactions, and the behavior that they engendered, affected and were affected by public policy. Private behavior was not directly shaped by government action, although the government was not without influence. As British historian J. R. Pole writes, with reference to the United States: "Government could not perhaps force [blacks and whites] to like each other, but it could ensure that equal opportunities were actually kept open. . . ."[11] While private conduct reflected concerns that did not routinely reach the policy level but were rather manifested in daily life, it had profound significance nonetheless. The revelation of aggregated individual social preferences in community behavior may be viewed as analogous to the economic preferences of individuals, as revealed in market behavior. Both the social and economic "markets" matter in their own right. And just as the aggregation of individual economic preferences is traditionally seen as interacting with and helping to shape public policy, so too private policy in the social realm influenced public decision making.

Private policy was not of a piece. On the one side, "strong subconscious resentment . . . at the loss of imperial grandeur"[12] was borne by the nonwhite arrivals, themselves tangible evidence of that altered national status. Not that these reactions to nonwhites were new to the British: with the appearance of nonwhites in Britain itself rather than in the colonies, they had just become more immediately realized and more consequential. As Anthony Lester and Geoffrey Bindman note: "Post-war immigration from the new Commonwealth has transplanted to the old mother country prejudices and patterns of behavior which could conveniently be ignored or righteously condemned so long as they flourished only within an Empire beyond our shores."[13] Pulling in the opposite direction was Britain's image of itself as a tolerant people, accepting of differences. The new immigrants put that self-perception to the sternest of tests.

Britain's response to the influx of former subjects from the Indian subcontinent and the Caribbean is, of course, too complicated a phenomenon to be understood by reference to any one event, even one so obviously laden with significance as the demise of Empire. The immigrants themselves, in all their diversity, importantly shape the tale. So too does the relationship between the new inequities of race and the hoary inequities inhering in the British social class system.[14] Tensions within the social welfare system between egalitarian and meritocratic goals, and between central and local government authorities as the appropriate determining agent of social policy goals, also contribute to the telling. It is a story of exquisite complexity, whose component parts have elsewhere been recounted in detail.[15] This chapter does not attempt to summarize those recountings, but rather highlights those aspects of the British experience that bear on the issues of educational policy and race with which we are chiefly concerned.

Inherent in educational policy are many of the dilemmas nascent in racial policy generally. To do right by the young West Indians, Pakistanis, and Indians was terribly important, at least for liberal-minded Britons in the 1960s. While the tensions between immigrant adults and the British could be attributed to the strains of newness, the persistence of inequity in the "second generation," Home Secretary Roy Jenkins declared, meant that "justice [would be] denied by the simple fact of skin pigmentation."[16] That was intolerable. The amelioration of those tensions, it was thought, required (among other things) that educational opportunities for nonwhites and whites be rendered equal, and in a more than formal sense. A familiar enough aspiration: how it assumed meaning, given the nature of the immigration, the reactions of the host society, and the capacities of the social service system in a nation that styled itself a social welfare state, constitutes our focus.

The New Immigrants. Only recently has Britain acquired a minority population of any size. Although Africans and Asians were familiar visitors in the nineteenth century, and the slaves of West Indian planters were routinely brought to England a century earlier, very few free nonwhites had ever settled in England. In 1951, some 75,000 Britons, less than two-tenths of one percent of the country's population, were of racial minority background. A decade later, after substantial immigration, just 7.3 persons per 1,000 of the population, most of them West Indians, were nonwhites born overseas.[17] While nonwhites are today a more substantially visible presence, their numbers—restricted by immigration laws passed since 1962—remain relatively small. In 1974, 1.6 million British residents, 2.9 percent of the population, were nonwhite.[18]

These new immigrants did not constitute a single group. If anything, they had rather more in common with the British than with each other. The chief distinction to be drawn is between the West Indians on the one hand, and the Indians, Bangladeshis, and Pakistanis on the other; these aggregations, themselves composed of diverse communities, differed in terms of language, culture, history, and skin color. Their most important common attributes were that they were new to Britain and were not white.

The aspirations of these two groups of arrivals were quite distinct. While both West Indians and Indian subcontinent immigrants hoped for a better life in England, they held divergent views of what that good life constituted. The Indians and Pakistanis were and have remained economic migrants, interested in Britain primarily for the material prosperity it could bring to them, not at all anxious to become British. However fanciful the notion may now be, most Indians and Pakistanis still cling to the hope of eventually returning to the home country.[19] In the meantime, they have sought to preserve the village, kin, and organizational structures they brought with them, wanting above all to be left alone by their hosts. Not so the West Indians, who at least in the early years of migration saw themselves as Englishmen.

As one spokesman noted: "We are not immigrants in the true technical sense: after all, we are members of the realm, we are British."[20] The West Indians' behavior confirmed this view. They tried to adjust to British ways, marrying earlier, restricting the size of their families, and (despite their living in crime-prone areas) maintaining lower crime rates than the native British population. This difference in aspiration stemmed in part from the kind of culture that the West Indian, as distinguished from the Indian or Pakistani, had left, a culture that made identification as British at least a plausible illusion. As Catherine Jones observes:

> To talk of a West Indian culture was, in a sense, to talk of an artifact in which things European, things African, things Asian, things Oriental, and of course things British were all variously to be traced, yet all subtly modified by their particular island contexts . . . . So composite and varied an inheritance could at once provide points of affinity, and immigrant expectations of affinity, with British society and, at the same time, furnish ample proofs of differences between host and colonial (or ex-colonial) norms.
>
> The scope for such mutual misunderstanding was less apparent in the Indian and Pakistani case. Moslem, Sikh or Hindu allegiances, for instance, amounted to far more recognizable, predictable, and internally consistent patterns of behavior . . . for the host society to come to terms with.[21]

Coming to terms with an influx of newcomers was difficult for a people often criticized for its "insular arrogance."[22] That these newcomers were both strange, even as compared with the earlier waves of Irish and Jewish immigrants, and readily identifiable, compounded matters. If the mass arrivals were not traceable to "a fit of absence of mind"[23] on the part of the British—private employers, for example had actively recruited nonwhite labor—their arrival nevertheless caught the country unawares. There were no prophets to anticipate that ex-colonials in substantial numbers would take seriously their right of citizenship; government officials did not accurately gauge either the need of postwar British industry for cheap, unskilled labor that the immigrants could satisfy or the capacity of the colonial communities to organize migration.[24]

Beginning in the mid-1950s, the Home Office did keep track of the number of what were euphemistically termed "New Commonwealth Immigrants." Through the balance of the decade, the government attempted with little success to limit those numbers through bilateral agreements with the sending nations. By 1958, when race riots in Nottingham[25] and Notting Hill forcibly called attention to the immigrants, it was seemingly too late for Britain to reverse course, even if the nation had wanted to do so. Lord Gardiner, Lord Chancellor in Harold Wilson's first administration, declared to the House of Lords: "The actions, or rather the inaction, of the past two administrations mean that neither our children nor their children will ever see the England which we have been used to seeing, because for good or ill England has become a multi-racial society."[26]

The apparent inadvertence of the immigration, coupled with its consequential impact, was subsequently deployed to rationalize a demand for the repatriation of the nonwhite immigrants. As Enoch Powell argued, in a 1971 speech: "No government has the right to alter the character and identity of a nation without the nation's knowledge and without that nation's will."[27]

Legacy of Empire: Insularity and Superiority

The Relevance of History. The colonial experience did not prepare the British to cope well with the strains of a multi-racial society. Quite the contrary:

British insularity was said to preclude "not only fusion, but also sympathy and almost intercourse with the subject races."[28] Britain's attempt to introduce India to the best of European civilization was rudely interrupted by the 1857 revolt, an event described by Sir John Lawrence, Governor of India, as nothing less than a "war of races."[29] Thereafter, the British presence was somewhat more circumspect, their contact with Indians more restricted. The British did, of course, co-opt and Anglicize some of the Indian elite; for the most part, however, they maintained both their distance and their sense of superiority. "Englishmen like posing as Gods," as E. M. Forster observed in *A Passage to India*.[30] Even as he sought to put the best possible light on the Indian colonial experience, James Bryce, writing at the turn of the century, stressed both the separation between the individual Indian and Briton, and the sense of British superiority. Britain had ruled "a subject race on principles of strict justice," keeping order "in an immense population standing on a lower plane of civilization." Added Bryce: "[T]he existence of a system securing these benefits is compatible with an *absolute separation between the rulers and the ruled*."[31]

In the West Indies, both planters and missionaries developed a paternalistic intimacy with the islanders, growing in part out of the master-slave relationships of the eighteenth century,[32] which had no counterpart in India. But the eventual British disillusionment with the West Indians, stemming from a revolt in Jamaica in 1865, seems much the same; so too was a hardening of the British heart toward an ungrateful subject people. As *The Times* editorialized, in the aftermath of revolt:

> Though a fleabite compared with the Indian mutiny, [the Jamaica revolt] touches our pride more and is more in the nature of a disappointment. . . . Jamaica is our pet institution, and its inhabitants are our spoilt children. . . . It seemed to be proved in Jamaica that the negro could become fit for self government. . . . Alas for grand triumphs of humanity

> and the improvement of races, and the removal of primeval curses, and the expenditure of twenty millions sterling, Jamaica herself gainsays the fact and belies herself, as we see today.[33]

These recountings are vast oversimplifications, to be sure. Yet they hint at a tendency of British colonial rule: a special kind of paternalism, premised not on personal understanding, as parents feel for their children, but on the invention of an idealized subject people, "Calibans and Ariels"[34] whom Englishmen could care for. The invention inevitably collapsed, as the West Indian and Indian asserted their personhood, but the presumption of British superiority precluded understanding, let alone taking seriously, the real and expressed wishes of the colonized. "As soon as one of the natives ventured to ask for independence or freedom he became 'disloyal' or (more recently) an extremist."[35]

This tendency to link isolation with assertions of British superiority persisted until the end of Empire, even if political etiquette precluded giving it full voice. The lawn party that opens *A Passage to India* captures the nature of the relationship. One Englishwoman, a longtime inhabitant of India, is asked by a newcomer to the country to introduce her to the Indian ladies gathered uncomfortably on one quarter of the grounds. " 'You're superior to them, anyway. Don't forget that. You're superior to everyone in India except one or two of the Ranis, and they're on an equality.' "[36] The ensuing exchange between the Indian and English ladies is stilted; how could it be otherwise, when there is no fabric to their relationship, only this occasion. And how like a Jamaican's description, written four decades later, of the contacts between nonwhites newly arrived in England and their liberal white greeters. "[O]n kiddies' chairs . . . the middle class elite, MPs, reverends and idealists . . . unblinkingly faced the robustness of the migrants, and with their beautiful English manners politely observed the invisible gulf which existed between themselves and their dark brothers."[37]

The sense of British superiority underlying Bryce's reference to the Indians as "standing on a lower plane of civilization" finds its contemporary confirmation in British attitudes. In a 1967 poll, more than three-fifths of those surveyed stated that they regarded themselves as superior to Africans and Asians (a handful, less than 4 percent, viewed the British as inferior).[38] The Africans' and Asians' relative lack of education and the cultural differences between the peoples were the stated causes of this feeling of superiority. The persistence of such views reflects and reveals British private policy; it suggests that the British could only be most ambivalent hosts to the nonwhite immigrants.

This is not how Britons view the matter. They regard themselves as an extremely tolerant people vigorously opposed to racism. Sociologist Michael Banton, writing in the 1950s, detected a widely suffused norm of tolerance; only 2 percent of the British, he concluded, could be described as strongly racially prejudiced.[39] Of the more than three-fifths of Britons who, in the 1967 survey, regarded the British as a superior people, less than 5 percent attributed this superiority to race.[40] Subsequent polls report that no more than one in ten Englishmen can properly be characterized as actively hostile to the nonwhite immigrants.[41] "The English people," as Ann Dummett writes, "are accustomed to thinking of racism as a Bad Thing, but they are convinced that it is always happening somewhere else."[42]

The American Contrast. This self-image with respect to issues of race stands in marked contrast to that of the United States. In *An American Dilemma*, Gunnar Myrdal described the profound tension between the egalitarian "American creed," on the one hand, and the inferior treatment of blacks on the other. "*The need for race prejudice is, from this point of view, a need for defense on the part of the Americans against their own national Creed, against their own most cherished ideals.*"[43] That tension was exacerbated by the dramatic events of the 1950s and 1960s: the authoritative declaration in the 1954 *Brown* decision that racial segregation was unlawful, the determinedly nonviolent efforts of blacks to assert their claim to equality under the American creed, and the violence of Southern white repression of those efforts.

Seen in this perspective, the revolution in American civil rights policy and the no less revolutionary changes in American private policy, as embodied in whites' actions and attitudes, that have occurred in the past three decades represent the gradual and far from complete triumph of a moral imperative, as embodied in the egalitarian national self-image. As Myrdal among many others had pointed out, Americans long knew that they had treated blacks badly. Once that knowledge became intolerable, the nation set out, however falteringly, to confront the awful legacy of its own history. J. R. Pole concludes: "When the American situation as it was . . . even as late as . . . 1945, is compared with that of [the 1970s] . . . the difference to be observed amounts to a far greater transformation both in the distribution of opportunity and the obligations of government than in any period that had occurred since the American Revolution."[44]

In Britain, matters were very different—a point the British were fond of reiterating. Unlike the United States, Britain had no deep and scarring history of racial exploitation at home. Slavery in Britain, never significant, had long since vanished. There existed no explicit legal racial disabilities to undo. The colonies were far away, and a distinguishable matter besides. There is a British counterpart to the American dilemma—the gap between a self-image of tolerance and the reality of the shabby treatment accorded to those viewed as racial (or social class) inferiors—but it was less widely appreciated. There is just enough truth in the image of tolerance to render silly blunt assaults on British racism, and subtler propositions are harder to press.

The Policy Response. This national difference has profound significance for policy, public and private. Change in both the private and public spheres is most likely when there exists consensus that the *status quo* can no longer be endured; change comes hardest when present arrangements seem perfectly acceptable. In Britain, there is not—or until very recently was not—much sense of a "problem," and hence little support for trying some new remedy.

Cures that involved changing the British themselves—whether these took the form of antidiscrimination legislation, conciliation efforts, or redistribution of resources from whites to nonwhites—were seen as at best unnecessary, at worst harmful to the promotion of race relations. If anything was needed, it was time. Ann Dummett quotes a frequently voiced British viewpoint:

> If only the newspapers and television would stop harping on race, if only they'd just *keep quiet*, it would all get better, wouldn't it? It only needs time. You can't expect people to get used to coloured people just overnight, can you? But British people are very fair: if the newspapers would only stop, we could get on very quietly with living together.[45]

The nonwhites also needed time to adjust to British mores. To that end, the liberal-minded British were willing to be of help. A multitude of liaison committees, local friendship councils, Anglo-Indian and Anglo-Caribbean social clubs, and intercultural events were all testimony to this reaching out.

Occasionally, as with the 1958 race riots, a less patient and tolerant face of Britain was visible. Lord Justice Salmon's condemnation of several young whites convicted for assaulting West Indians in Notting Hill came to symbolize the dominant British view of the matter.

> You are a minute and insignificant section of the population who have brought shame on the district in which you lived, and have filled the whole nation with horror, indignation and disgust. Everyone, irrespective of the colour of their skin, is entitled to walk through our streets with heads erect and free from fear.[46]

The Lord Justice's opinion confirmed the national sense of fairness, even while dismissing racial violence as aberrant behavior.

The more considered reaction to the riots, and more generally to pervasive unease about the pace (if not the fact) of immigration, was somewhat different. Fair treatment for the newcomer was the touchstone of private policy, at least among the liberal-minded. It might be appropriate to go farther than this, and make fairness—nondiscrimination—the basis for public policy as well. This was only possible, however, if the rate of immigration was slowed sufficiently to minimize the perception of threat that the newcomers evidently conveyed, thus enabling the British to adjust more gradually and gracefully to their altered circumstances. In failing to limit nonwhite immigration and attempting to deal fairly with all the new immigrants, Britain had apparently asked too much of itself.

Immigration restrictions, anathema to Labourites and liberal Tories as late as 1960, shortly thereafter became consensual policy, transcending party lines. Subsequent Labour support for restrictive legislation prompted the *Economist* to note that, on this issue, the party had "pinched the Tories' white trousers."[47] Almost simultaneously there came the first glimmerings of a realization on the part of liberal members of both parties that private policy alone was not enough: racial justice at home was also properly within the province of government.

The link between immigration curbs and a domestic racial policy was explicitly forged, as politicians concluded that British popular concerns relating to immigration were not necessarily racist. Roy Hattersley, the Labour M.P., declared that "without integration, limitation is inexcusable; without limitation, integration is impossible."[48] The standard-bearer for British liberalism on this question, the then Home Secretary, Roy Jenkins, said much the same: "Immigration should not be so high as to create a widespread resistance to effective integration policies [nor] so unreasonably low as to create an embittered sense of grievance in the immigrant community itself."[49] With the passage of the first immigrant control legislation and the adoption of weak antidiscrimination legislation early in the 1960s, Britain had officially admitted to the presence of a dilemma.

Speaking in 1966 to the House of Lords, Lord Stonham praised the undertaking. "We shall make a great success of this policy—a success which, I think, will be an example to the world."[50] Yet Britain had little experience with public policy aimed directly at the alleviation of social conflict, and in this area there was every reason for skepticism. Private policy, the sum of individuals' attitudes and practices, had neither accepted the existence of a problem, nor put much stock in a governmental solution.

Race Policy: Promoting Nondiscrimination and Racial Harmony

Public policy responses to the immigrant issue assumed two forms: efforts to improve relationships between the races and proscriptions against discrimination. The aspiration was to promote interracial harmony in the long run, while undoing discrimination in the present. In practice, both undertakings proved problematic.

Community Relations. Improving relationships between whites and nonwhites, the goal of community relations policy, presumes that there exists a vision of Britain to which both groups aspire. By the mid–1960s, this commonality of vision was lacking. While the British remained ready to accept immigrants who would assimilate British ways, the immigrants no longer seemed so accommodating. Insofar as one could speak of an immigrant point of view, it was embodied in their desire to preserve distinct identities, to be accepted "as they were, rather than as they might become, given suitable instruction,"[51] a prospect which, by definition, required adjustments on the part of the hosts as well as the newcomers. This was not what the majority of British people understood tolerance to demand.

The aim of a community relations effort was thus murky. Murkier yet were the means of going about the task. The Community Relations Commission created by the 1968 Race Relations Act had little power to act, only the capacity to reason and persuade. Was it to exercise this capacity on behalf of a nonwhite clientele, pressing that constituency's concerns upon other branches of government? Or was it instead to serve as the voice of government, conveying official policy to the nonwhite community?[52] Was it, in matters of substance, to encourage assimilation or ethnic diversity? With such profound uncertainties with respect to ends and means, goals and strategies, the enterprise was doomed from the start, whatever it did. That indeed was the widespread assessment of the commission's work, upon its absorption into the Commission for Racial Equality in 1977. Only reluctantly was it acknowledged that its numerous publications, conferences, gadfly activities, and quiet good works were not without value.

Local community relations councils, established throughout the country to address race in the particular and concrete, have suffered an even worse time. The councils are neither community action agencies, in the model of the American "war on poverty" agencies of the 1960s, nor providers of substantial social services. In an inherently controversial realm, they have generally tried to be noncontroversial and constructive. Their critics on the right oppose any unbecoming partisan efforts on their part. Their critics on the left perceive them as extending a measure of paternalistic patronage to docile middle-class nonwhites, while serving essentially as a buffer between nonwhites and the British political system.[53]

Nondiscrimination. In contrast with improving community relations, combatting racial discrimination seems a relatively clear-cut goal. The mechanism chosen for this purpose, administrative and judicial review, had been used for broadly similar ends with somewhat encouraging results in the United States.[54] Lord Justice Salmon's statement in the Notting Hill riot case embodied a reminder that the law served in Britain as a profoundly important symbol of fairness.

Despite this more auspicious background, the antidiscrimination efforts too have to be reckoned problematic. Despite reliable evidence of widespread discrimination, especially with respect to housing and employment, the number of discrimination cases brought to the Race Relations Board, the body created by the 1968 Race Relations Act to address these issues, has been relatively low: 1,138 in 1975, the last year for which figures are available.[55] Many of these complaints raised issues of relatively trivial importance, such as denial of admission to dance halls. Almost none posed issues generalizable to large numbers of nonwhites. While the board possessed the legal authority to seek out significant instances of discrimination on its own initiative, without waiting for a complaint, this power went nearly unused.

The board's stated preference was to resolve cases through conciliation, rather than by force of law. Of the 1,083 cases disposed of in 1975, the board concluded that there had been unlawful discrimination in 233. Of these, conciliation—tried in all instances—failed in some 97 cases. The board determined to take 45 of the disputes to court—15 more than in any previous year. Only 13 cases actually reached the courts.

In part, this preference for a nonjudicial approach is attributable to the board's mixed record of judicial successes, itself indicative of basic differences between the American and British judicial approaches to the issue of discrimination. American courts have in general adopted an expansive view of those constitutional and statutory provisions designed to secure racial nondiscrimination. By contrast, the British courts have not read the Race Relations Act broadly, as a charter for racial justice. They have been rather more inclined to narrow the scope of the act; perhaps the best example of this is a House of Lords decision that discrimination against a Pole did not constitute discrimination on the impermissible basis of "national origin" but rather discrimination on the supposedly different basis of nationality, to which the act did not speak.[56]

The Race Relations Board and its liberal supporters attributed this relatively weak performance to a lack of certain formal legal powers in the 1968 legislation. The 1976 Race Relations Act corrects these alleged flaws, and also creates a new Commission for Racial Equality to undertake both community relations and antidiscrimination activities. Yet the source of the board's problems lies less with any lack of formal authority than with the lack of fit between a legislative approach to racial issues and the British legal and social environment. Civil rights legislation, vigorously enforced by the courts, was a natural legal development in the United States. American courts had a lengthy acquaintanceship with policy setting; as Alexis de Tocqueville had long ago observed, in *Democracy in America:* "Scarcely any political question arises . . . that is not resolved, sooner or later, into a judicial question."[57] And racial justice was thought to be a fit subject for judicial activism. Indeed, the courts had expressly evinced a special solicitude for the plight of what one Supreme Court justice termed "discrete and insular minorities."[58] In Britain, by contrast, the courts' role in policy making has historically been modest, and significant racial questions had not come before the judiciary since the famous emancipation cases some two centuries earlier.[59] Under these circumstances, there was about as much reason to believe that the transplant of American civil rights law would take root in Britain as to believe that California avocados could be raised equally well in Cornwall.

Conciliation could not achieve much in a society whose members were unpersuaded that they should alter their view of what constituted good race relations by accommodating to nonwhites. Those who questioned prevailing norms were regarded as a combination of "the unbalanced, the unrealistic, the gullible—if not, in the last resort, the unpatriotic."[60] The mere venting of discrimination as an issue led one former city councillor to accuse Nottingham's Anti-Colour Bar Campaign of stirring up racial hatred, in violation of the race relations legislation.[61] Antidiscrimination efforts "had been attacked . . . from the outset as being, on the one hand yet another invasion of the individual's sacred liberty and, on the other, a wholly impracticable, pointless manoeuvre."[62] Disbelief in the prevalence of discrimination in a nation that perceived itself as fundamentally fair-minded and tolerant persisted despite evidence to the contrary. For that reason, "the introduction of antidiscrimination legislation amounted, allegedly, to no more than a short-sighted, gratuitous attack upon native sentiments and freedoms."[63]

Social Welfare Policy: Universalism and Special Needs

Policies which addressed racial issues directly, whether through suasion or force of law, remained to the popular mind cures in search of a malady whose significance, indeed whose very existence, was not appreciated. Efforts to address racial issues less directly, through social welfare support, presented quite distinct if no less troublesome questions. Britain in the late 1950s and 1960s styled itself a welfare state, one which assumed some collective responsibility for the well-being of all its inhabitants. "The Welfare State," as Catherine Jones states, "was nothing if not committed to the idea of fundamental common interest and obligation."[64] This was a new and rather startling development; it was also one whose contours were, at best, imperfectly defined.

The arrival of large numbers of nonwhite immigrants tested both the institutional capacity and the ideological underpinnings of the system. How did the sense of "fundamental common interest and obligation" relate to immigrant needs? On the one hand, for government not to recognize the immigrants' particular needs—instruction in English, for example—meant that this clientele would not be well served. As a group, nonwhites were in certain respects different from the indigenous population. They were, on the average, poorer and employed in lower status jobs than whites; they did less well in school; they lived in more crowded and more run-down housing. The sources of their disadvantage were to some extent unique: education, for example, was worth less to nonwhites, in terms of income benefits, than to whites. Because race reaches so many aspects of an individual's life, it seemed likely that these problems, if unresolved, would affect succeeding generations. As David Smith notes in *Racial Disadvantage in Britain*, "there can be virtually no mobility, even between generations, across racial boundaries, as was possible across social class boundaries. If therefore particular racial groups come to be identified with an inferior role in society, then this will tend to persist indefinitely."[65] In short, unless specially helped, nonwhites could conceivably become a permanent underclass.

On the other hand, to single out nonwhites for special treatment risked charges of favoritism, and might well pit the needy against one another. Moreover, Britons did not regard this group as having a particular claim on the public fisc. The dilemmas of social class were familiar; the unique dilemmas of race were not generally acknowledged. Nor was it clear that some race-specific efforts could effectively respond to many nonwhites' needs. Beyond instruction in English, what race-specific undertakings made sense?

Even if racial minorities merited special attention in the welfare state, it by no means followed that a uniform policy, administered and controlled by the national government, was appropriate. A great many social services in Britain are decentralized in their administration, including those with most obvious relevance to the new immigrants: housing, social welfare, employment, and education. To a considerable extent, this decentralization is the preferred governance structure for central as well as local government. Government departments, far from seeking to expand their domain, seem sometimes to take a positive delight in the narrow scope of their power.

Throughout the early 1960s, the central government routinely stated that immigrant issues were local issues and could be dealt with competently at that level. When, beginning with the Local Government Act in 1966, the national government first began distributing money on the basis of numbers of nonwhites, it left most decisions concerning its expenditure to local authorities. While the more ambitious 1968 Urban Programme, the most recent legislative social initiative, was by British standards closely managed from Whitehall, it preserved far more local government choice than, say, the American Model Cities and Community Action programs of the 1960s.

These related disagreements concerning the special character of nonwhite needs and the wisdom of a national view on the matter rendered the national government understandably cautious. The natural tendency was to diminish the significance of race, to act insofar as was possible without explicit attention to race by noting the shared and nonracial vulnerabilities of needy people. In part, this was a political response: race was a kind of social dynamite, explosive if not handled gingerly. Inexplicitness was also an ideologically driven response.

> The whole philosophy of the Welfare State . . . had hitherto seemed to centre around the idea of catering for certain categories of social need irrespective of "extraneous" social, cultural, or economic personal characteristics. To treat, or even to record, coloured immigrants differently, for no other reason than because they were coloured immigrants, seemed to strike at the heart of this philosophy, and to constitute a form of colour discrimination which, whether it was intended to be positive or negative in the first instance, seemed a highly dangerous and unwelcome precedent.[66]

Paradoxically, in America the legislation that outlawed discrimination legitimated the very kinds of racial specificity that so troubled the British: racial tabulations, which had commonly been illegal prior to the 1964 Civil Rights Act, which outlawed racial discrimination, were subsequently widely required. Although America has not fully come to terms with the implications of preferential treatment of any sort for nonwhites, let alone the much stickier issue of preferential racial quotas, such preferences have become commonplace throughout a wide range of government-administered programs.[67]

British social services took a quite different position.[68] For some services, such as welfare (National Insurance), the irrelevance of race was easily enough maintained; money is, after all, money. Agencies that provided services, however, had a more difficult time. Particular local authority health checks, for example, could be attacked as discriminatory because they specially singled out nonwhite immigrants. In trying to match would-be workers and jobs, the employment services had to worry about the possibility of discrimination (as well as the resentment of employers toward " 'unreliable [nonwhite] workers and spongers' ").[69] Housing agencies' policies could be decried as discriminatory, even if scrupulously nonracial, when they resulted in the provision of less adequate public housing to nonwhites than whites.[70] Because education authorities are in the business of shaping character, whatever stance they took toward race had relevance for policy, even if their posture was studiously to ignore the subject. Whether educators sought to assimilate nonwhite youngsters into the British mainstream, or instead to manage a truce between races and cultures, the decision was question raising.

Housing, education, and employment agencies possess the potential power to encourage racial mixing; in fact, because three Britons in ten live in public housing, and because direct government involvement in the economy is substantial, the possibility for government action in these domains is greater than in the United States. In some instances, integration was quietly and inexplicitly undertaken. Students were dispersed to white schools and nonwhite families to white housing estates; and some employment services sought to place racial minority workers in hitherto all-white firms. But these were the apparent exceptions. Supplying homes, schooling, and jobs, within a framework which gave choices to both nonwhites and whites, was more generally deemed the primary task of the government agency. Where the agencies did attempt to foster racial mixing, they were at pains not to be looked upon as doing so. For the most part, the social services deemphasized the specialness of their new clientele, even as they recognized the limitations of this approach. As one social care agency stated: "It is the Department's responsibility to provide an individualized service for everyone. This includes immigrants on the same basis as everyone else, even though they might call for *more* individualized or more exceptional treatment."[71] A considerable achievement—if the social welfare system could manage it.

The Invisible Minority

In the United States, blacks had a significant say in the shaping of 1960s civil rights policies, and through the community action program entered seriously into the realm of social welfare policy making.[72] Not so in Britain, where the legacy of paternalism and distance keeping held sway. Nonwhites have been the intended beneficiaries of governmental action, not partners in its crafting. They have been treated as patients, not agents. The benefits of inexplicitness were extolled by whites on behalf of an imagined clientele, not asserted by the racial minority leadership.

An Antiguan who visited England a century ago warned the British that nonwhite colonials "would one day seek to avenge the insults and oppression they experienced" as sojourners in Britain.[73] While there is as yet little indication of that happening, increasing support for racial separatism on the part of vocal leadership is observable. The West Indian spokesmen, initially willing to accept British guidance, abandoned that stance in the face of disillusionment with the treatment they actually received. As one West Indian declared: "The British people whom I and the rest of us met [in the West Indies] were to us paragons of everything manly, courageous, wonderful. How can I or any other West Indian live down this great lie?"[74] Beginning in the late 1950s, the attitude of West Indian organizations shifted "away from assimilation and multi-racialism, towards self-help and emphasis on a distinct West Indian identity."[75] A West Indian reporting on the situation at the end of the 1960s reached a similar conclusion: "Most West Indian organizations oscillate between rejection, root and branch, of the 'host society,' and a search to make the best of its better radical tradition."[76] Public expressions of hostility have persisted in the intervening decade.[77]

The Indian, Bangladeshi, and Pakistani communities historically had less contact with the British, and thus were less susceptible to their influence, than were the West Indians. When queried, very few thought that emulation of British ways was either beneficial or very likely to happen.[78] This practice of self-imposed isolation has persisted, indeed been cultivated, despite the fact that most of the Indians and Pakistanis now in Britain may perforce be regarded as permanent British citizens. The self-reliance of certain of these Indian subcontinent communities may even be growing: when confronted by white violence and ineffective peace keeping by police, the Bangladeshis of East London began to form their own defense groups. To judge from the public rhetoric, the nonwhite viewpoint approaches that expressed by Dr. Aziz, in *A Passage to India*: "The approval of your [British] compatriots no longer interests me; I have become anti-British, and ought to have done so sooner, it would have saved me numerous misfortunes."[79]

These observations concerning nonwhite attitudes are only best guesses whose significance should not be exaggerated. For one thing, they do not take into account the generally more positive surveys of individual opinion.[80] For another, the absence of both an enduring and energetic nonwhite leadership willing to deal with the larger society and of strong links between the nonwhite communities and their white allies makes generalizations about the minority groups' perceptions—risky business at the best of times—particularly hazardous in this instance. The West Indian community appears from the outside to be unformed and even inchoate; most of its members belong to no group and the voices that are heard do not seem to command general respect. (Perhaps the most influential nonwhite voice ever to be raised in Britain was that of an American, Martin Luther King.) While the Indian subcontinent communities are far better organized, they have not sought linkages with white Britain, but instead have concentrated their energies on self-help efforts. The Committee against Racial Discrimination (CARD) tried to bring together a wide range of minority groups and liberal white supporters, but that enterprise literally split itself apart in the late 1960s.[81] There is nothing in Britain that can remotely be compared with the National Association for the Advancement of Colored People (NAACP).

A quarter-century in Britain has not molded West Indian, Pakistani, and Indian into a single group. That they have been commonly referred to as "coloured" only indicates the host country's insensitivity to racial nuance. Today, "coloured" is viewed in certain quarters as insulting; it has some of the same connotations as "Negro" in the United States. They are no longer "New Commonwealth Immigrants," as the government used to call them: well over half of the nonwhite population below age 16 was born in Britain. Some self-appointed spokesmen have insisted upon "black" as a mark of their shared oppression at the hands of white England.[82] The label must be appreciated in ideological terms, as a reaction against assimilation and an attempt to make common cause against whites; for "black" (rather like "coloured") denies the tug of culture and history, to say nothing of the reality of skin color.[83] It is as if, in the United States, the Latino and Native American communities were to identify themselves as black. If indeed "black" becomes common coin in Britain, this fact may presage a new stage in British race relations. For the moment, however, the dominant motifs seem to be an uneasy paternalism on the one side, a quiet hostility on the other.

The Race Policy Conundrum

The nonwhite presence raises several broad social policy questions, each of exquisite difficulty. What public policy stance should be adopted with respect to racial issues, where the very existence of a racial problem is widely disputed, at least in the private sphere? Which if any of the nonwhite population's special needs should be recognized in crafting a social welfare policy (and with what likelihood of satisfying that special need)? How, if at all, should nonwhite aspirations, with respect both to particular substantive policies and participation in their shaping, be taken into account by those charged with directing British policy?

Each of these nettlesome questions has surfaced repeatedly, in the context of particular policy puzzles. In this sense, educational policy—the focus of the inquiry—is significant both in its own right and as emblematic of a more generic policy process.

two

The Evolution of British Race and Schooling Policy

Race in the Educational Policy Context

Between 1960 and the early 1970s, British primary and secondary schools became significantly multiracial. The nonwhites who had just come to Britain entered an educational system struggling with two related issues. There existed a substantive tension between the abstract tugs of egalitarianism and elitism, and—differently—diversity and uniformity: in concrete form, this was embodied in the protracted political dispute over comprehensive secondary schooling. Also detectable was a structural tension between long-dominant localism and the hesitant claims of the Department of Education and Science (DES) for national policy-making authority in certain areas. Although these concerns, at least as they were initially formulated, had no direct relationship to race, both the structural and the substantive conflicts helped to shape the educational system's response to its new clientele. It is these matters to which we turn first.

The appearance of nonwhites also trailed in its wake many of the issues that have come to be associated with the American race and schooling experience. The relationship between that fact and the reception accorded the racial minorities is more obvious and will occupy the bulk of our attention.

Inegalitarianism and Localism

The British educational system was, until recently, overtly structured along social class lines, providing very different kinds of education to rich children and poor children. Had the nonwhites arrived with the Irish a century earlier, they probably would have enjoyed only so much education as they could pay for or supply themselves; free education, even in the rudiments, was the exception. Even had they come just before the onset of World War II, nonwhites would in all likelihood have joined the great majority of Britons who went directly from school to factory or mine at age fourteen.[1] At the time they did arrive, however, differentiation within the educational system, especially differentiation that effectively distinguished along social class lines, had come sharply under attack. The nonwhites, who needed some differentiated assistance and who (over time) claimed a right to equal treatment, had somehow to be fitted into the larger ongoing debate.

Those who, in the first half of the nineteenth century, undertook to offer education to indigent British children had a clear sense of what they were about. It was important that the newly enfranchised poor be able to exercise their powers of citizenship responsibly, and literacy was central to that end. "We must compel our future Masters to learn their letters," as Robert Lowe, Vice President of the Committee of the Privy Council on Education, remarked.[2] But the education received by the poor would be unmistakeably different from that available to the upper classes:

> The lower classes ought to be educated to discharge the duties cast upon them. They should also be educated that they may appreciate and defer to the higher cultivation when they meet it, and the higher classes ought to be educated in a very different manner in order that they may exhibit to the lower classes that higher education to which, if it were shown to them, they would bow down and defer.[3]

The view that education was vital to the development of a responsible but subservient class also prevailed with respect to education in the colonies during the nineteenth century. It was the hope of enlightened British colonialists in Asia and the Caribbean that schooling the nonwhite population would promote their "moral and intellectual emancipation."[4] "Emancipation" did not, however, mean intellectual or personal liberty, but rather the adoption of European standards. Education was a socially conservative undertaking because "the educated [native] was a loyal subject";[5] or so it was commonly supposed, even if in practice education seemed to engender dissatisfaction as often as loyalty.

Mid-nineteenth century England knew an alternative view. It was borrowed from the American experience with common schools, and pressed by such radical leaders as Richard Cobden:

> Notwithstanding the great gulf that separates the middle from the working classes and the middle from the higher classes in this country, nothing would tend so much to break down that barrier as to erect common schools of so superior a quality that people should find nowhere in their vicinity an opportunity—whatever the class might be—of giving the children a better opportunity than by availing themselves of the facilities afforded by the common schools.[6]

That was not the end that British educational policy was to pursue. The first major legislation, the 1870 act, while providing for government support of some elementary schools, preserved a dual educational system. The state-supported schools were essentially poor schools; children of the wealthier classes attended either endowed grammar or newly created secondary schools, both of which operated primary classes. Beyond the primary level, only those who could pay the school fees could attend. As the 1870 act's draftsman observed, the legislation did not rework the basic system but instead "filled the gaps" in school provision.[7]

Although the 1902 act laid the foundation for a national secondary school system, reserving one-quarter of the places in secondary schools for the deserving poor, it maintained the distinction between elementary and secondary systems. Poor children continued to get far less education than the well off. As late as 1938, four out of every five British youngsters left school at age fourteen; of those, more than a third attended only all-age elementary schools, which were not equipped to offer any advanced programs.[8] H. C. Dent, editor of the *Times Educational Supplement,* excoriated the then prevailing system as "both quantitatively and qualitatively grossly inadequate to meet the needs of a democracy," representing instead "the very essence of inequality of opportunity. It is socially stratified to a degree that would be ludicrous were it not so tragic."[9]

The 1944 Education Act, which remains the charter for British education, redressed many of the then prevailing inequities. Not that the inequities were treated as such: "In characteristically English fashion all the various arguments about equality in education concentrated on practical issues; and although it was a subject that lent itself to abstract philosophizing, that was not the way in which war-time Britain approached it."[10] The 1944 act provided universal secondary education to age sixteen, abolished fees in state-maintained schools, and ended the distinction between the elementary and secondary educational systems. It also substantially increased the authority lodged in the central government.

What kind of secondary education would be provided by the local authorities, watched over by the education ministry? The legislation itself speaks of "such variety of instruction and training as may be desirable in view of [the students'] different ages, abilities, and aptitudes. . . ." In practice, this translated into a three-tier secondary system—grammar, technical, and secondary modern schools—with assignment to one or another school dependent on performance on the "eleven plus" examinations. "Selection by differentiation takes the place of selection by elimination":[11] the proposals of a government committee, advanced two decades earlier, had become policy. Almost from the outset, this arrangement provoked debate. An appointed commission attempted to rationalize the three-level arrangement by positing a like variety of students: "the pupil who is interested in learning for its own sake . . . the pupil whose interests and abilities lie markedly in the field of applied science or applied art . . . [and] the pupil who deals more easily with concrete things than with ideas."[12] That rationalization was ridiculed by educationists as presuming "that the Almighty has benevolently created three types of child in just those proportions which would gratify educational administrators."[13]

The tripartite secondary program and selection by early testing came under assault from various quarters. Some asserted on pedagogical grounds that the prevailing system "create[d] an artificial administrative barrier within what is essentially a single educational process. . . . 'There is or ought to be something for nearly everybody' in every school."[14] Sociologists, among them Jean Floud and A. H. Halsey, noted that existing arrangements served essentially to maintain social class disparities within the educational system.[15] The relatively weaker performance of poor children on the eleven-plus examination—attributable not to their lesser "innate" intelligence but to their relatively impoverished home backgrounds—also received attention, as did the unavoidable errors in judgment that crept into the examination system.

On their own—indeed, sometimes against the express views of DES—local authorities began abolishing separate grammar and secondary modern schools and moving toward a comprehensive secondary system. By 1962, one out of every ten students was in a comprehensive or near-comprehensive program. Twelve years later, 71 percent of all authorities either already had or intended imminently to establish some form of comprehensive secondary education—this, after a Labour government had, in 1965, required all education authorities to end separatism in secondary education; its Tory successor had reversed field and ceased to press for comprehensive schooling; and Labour, returned to office, had revived the pressure and introduced legislation which would turn all state schools into comprehensive schools.[16]

At the same time, secondary education had become genuinely a part of the popular education system. Between 1950 and 1966, the number of children aged fifteen or older in full-time school attendance increased almost threefold, from 290,354 to 782,027 (the total school population was growing by only 24 percent). In 1964, almost 10 percent of youngsters aged seventeen and older were attending school full-time; thirteen years earlier, just 5.5 percent of this age group was in school.[17]

The expansion of educational opportunities was widely praised. Reliance on a comprehensive educational system, particularly insofar as it undermined the elite grammar schools, was a far more controversial proposition. Although comprehensive schooling had long been supported by the Labour Party, Harold Wilson assured teachers just before the 1964 election that grammar schools "would be abolished 'only over his dead body.'" As late as 1970, "[Wilson] was representing the comprehensive school as 'a grammar school for all.'"[18] Objections to the demise of grammar schools were—and remain—deeply felt. It was argued that this was the one public institution that rivalled the independent (public) schools, providing the kind of intellectual challenge to the brightest middle and working class students that a comprehensive school by its very nature could not offer. Were these beacons of educational excellence to be swallowed up by a public secondary system widely regarded as mediocre?

Other structural aspects of the new policy also occasioned consternation. Replacing the three-tiered system with a single school necessarily restricted parental choice, historically an important aspect of all British education legislation, including the 1944 Education Act. (Under the tripartite system, many more children sought a grammar school education than there were places available; in this sense, the choice formerly available was also restricted.) That the central government was insisting upon the shift to comprehensive schooling also provoked unhappiness among those who perceived a special source of strength in the localist tradition of British schools and the relative absence of a central guiding hand.

The transformation to a comprehensive secondary school system might produce greater equality—although on this point also there was room for debate. For some, the price to be paid was just too high. As the Conservative Minister of Education, Sir David Eccles, made the point some years earlier: "One must choose between justice and equality, for it is impossible to apply both principles at once. Those who support comprehensive schools prefer equality. Her Majesty's government prefer justice."[19]

Both the substantive debate over the wisdom of comprehensive schooling and the disputes between central and local authorities for the final say in the matter affected educational policy concerning nonwhite students. In substantive terms, it was hard to argue simultaneously for commonality of educational experience, the educational predicate for comprehensive schooling, and for the necessity of paying special attention to nonwhites. Putting to one side the generally conceded need to offer basic language instruction, were the nonwhites different from white students, in a way that secondary modern students and grammar students were not different? Why should race, but not social class or measured intelligence, be treated as relevant to policy? Of greater practical moment, the wisdom—even the political possibility—of substantial national educational policy initiatives with respect to nonwhites was limited by the pendency of the debate over comprehensive schooling. That question, not the treatment of nonwhites in Britain's schools, occupied center stage throughout the 1960s and early 1970s.[20] This was one factor among many that shaped DES's stance toward racial minorities.

The Racial Tinderbox

The changing racial composition of the British schools, and the perceived effect of that change on the character of the institutions, rendered race of policy relevance to educationists. Numbers tell part of the story. Between 1960 and 1972, the nonwhite student population—primarily composed of children of West Indian, Indian, Pakistani, African, and Asian immigrants—grew from an uncounted handful to 279,872, nearly 4 percent of the national total.[21] That population is concentrated in relatively few educational authorities. A majority of nonwhites attend school in the London metropolitan area, a great many of the rest in the industrial Midlands. As of 1970, half of Britain's 146 educational authorities remained essentially all white; some 24 authorities enrolled more than 7 percent nonwhite students. In a half-dozen authorities, all in or near London, one in every five students was nonwhite.

Because nonwhites tend to cluster in particular neighborhoods,[22] and hence attend the same schools, predominantly nonwhite schools do exist. Throughout Britain in 1970, 217 schools, less than 1 percent of the national total, were more than half black. By all accounts, both the absolute numbers of nonwhite students and the likelihood of their attending a predominantly nonwhite school have increased considerably in the intervening years.

Racial concentration does not inherently create problems. Related factors have, however, contributed to a sense of social unease. In several cities with sizable (and ever-growing) nonwhite student populations, whites have not hesitated to voice in clearly racial terms their discomfiture with the altered composition—and, as some would say, the altered character—of their schools. Suggestions first advanced in the early 1960s that nonwhites be schooled separately are now part of the platform of the small but noisy National Front.[23] Sporadic reports of physical violence directed toward Asian students—lunch money shakedowns, after-school bashings, and the like—underscore this nativist hostility. One study finds "a depressing amount of hostility in the attitudes of white students to their West Indian and Asian classmates."[24]

Racial tensions are not the only source of race-specific concern. By the early 1970s, assessments of student achievement confirmed the popular belief that nonwhites were not faring well in school. A national survey of teachers' impressions of racial minority performance concluded that nonwhites, particularly West Indians, were doing considerably worse than average.[25] Achievement test data collected by the Inner London Education Authority corroborated these impressions.[26] Only 8.1 percent of nonwhite students performed in the upper quartile; 53 percent were in the lowest quartile in tested English achievement. West Indian performance was somewhat worse than that of Pakistanis and Indians, but both fell substantially below the average: 57.9 percent of West Indians, 44.9 percent of Indians and Pakistanis, performed in the lowest quartile. In mathematics, where lack of fluency in English should have had less of a depressing effect on achievement, racial minority performance was actually slightly worse; here again, Asian students' achievement was marginally higher than that of West Indians. The lowest achievement scores were reported for nonwhites attending neighborhood schools more than 60 percent nonwhite: these students' reading scores were half a grade to a grade and a half below those of minority students attending 90 percent or more white schools.

The educational careers of nonwhite students seem to mirror their test performance. Proportionately few pursue studies beyond secondary school. At the other end of the educational spectrum, the situation is equally unhappy: West Indians are proportionately three and four times more likely than whites to be assigned to classes for the educationally subnormal.[27]

Racial concentration, interracial hostility, and poor minority academic performance: taken together, these constitute the plausible elements for a policy conflagration. The institutions directly concerned with race policy were not unaware of the situation. The Race Relations Board (now the Commission for Racial Equality), charged with rectifying discrimination—if necessary through court action—has responded to a variety of complaints alleging discrimination in education.[28] Liberal groups concerned with one or another aspect of race relations, ranging from the government-subsidized community relations organizations to privately funded research groups such as the Runnymede Trust, have addressed aspects of the issue. A parliamentary Select Committee on Race Relations and Immigration undertook three inquiries touching upon education policy between 1969 and 1977.[29] Less tangibly but no less significantly, there is a marked and growing recognition on the part of minority organizations that, as the West Indian Standing Committee stated, nonwhite children are getting a "raw deal" in the schools.

Despite these factors, race as such has had only modest impact on the British educational policy calculus. Little attention has been paid to the specific problem of nonwhite underachievement. Discrimination against nonwhites in school, the predicate for American judicial intervention, has until very recently been treated as irrelevant to Britain. The possibility that school authority actions—opening and closing schools, drawing attendance boundaries, and the like—"intentionally" separated nonwhite and white students has gone unexamined because to Britons it seems on its face incredible.[30] Indeed, it is intentional racial mixing that has been challenged as racially discriminatory—exactly the reverse of the American pattern.[31]

This last, however, is a development at the margin of policy. It constitutes an exception to the deliberate and sustained effort to treat inexplicitly with race. The aim of British policy has been, on the one hand, to stress the infinitely diverse needs of individual students, and, on the other, to imbed race in some broader policy context, such as educational disadvantage. In this sense, educational policy making has been consistent with policy making in other British social services, and very different from the American approach. So beside the point is race itself that, since 1972, the national government has collected no data that would permit estimation of even the number of nonwhite students. References to the shared difficulties or shared needs, if any, of that population are thus necessarily rooted in guess work.

What analysts are inclined to treat as coherent policy is often better depicted as a series of stays against confusion, *ad hoc* responses to circumstance. British reaction to student dispersal, or busing, for example, cannot be understood without reference to such immediate pressures. But in the main, British race and schooling policy has not been reflexive; nor can it be described as nonpolicy, a lapse of governmental attention. Quite the contrary: the deemphasis of the racial element, unwavering from almost the first days of racial conflict a decade and a half ago, has been deliberate. Inexplicitness has been the policy goal.

Whether this will continue to be the case is uncertain. The end of the 1970s may mark a British policy watershed concerning race. Some shift in viewpoint of British education policy makers, away from inexplicitness, is detectable. With the passage of the 1976 Race Relations Act, discrimination in education has acquired new legal significance; and DES plans to focus on West Indian underachievement. Even as American analysts of racial problems express their admiration for the British approach, whether through urging that a similar stance be adopted in the United States or, differently, through proposing reliance on the "pluralist political process,"[32] the British now contemplate embarking on a more explicit and more American-style race policy initiative. Policy ironies and, more important, policy dilemmas more vexing than either the Americans or the British appreciate are evidently at work here.

Language, Culture, Class—and Race

Beginning in the 1960s, the chief policy response to the increase in the proportion of nonwhites in British public schools was to define this group in nonracial terms, stressing instead some other characteristic. Throughout the 1960s, the most important of these characteristics were linguistic and cultural. Attention focused on the fact that this was a group of newcomers, unfamiliar (except for the West Indians) with the English language and innocent of British customs. In this perspective, the new arrivals were indistinguishable from the Cypriots and the Maltese who had come simultaneously (if in lesser numbers), not so different from the Jews who had arrived at the turn of the century, or even the Irish who had preceded them a century earlier.[33] In subsequent years, the educational disadvantage that this group shared with others, notably urban dwellers and the poor, became more salient. At neither time did the fact that these were nonwhite students assume especial relevance.

It was the nonwhite as non-English speaking who attracted initial and most sustained policy attention. Uniquely in the realm of what might be broadly termed race and schooling policy, the central government offered both guidance and money to ensure instruction in English. DES's initial foray into the field was *English for Immigrants,*[34] a pamphlet asserting that special instruction by specially trained teachers was essential if the non-English speaking were to perform well in school. Variations of that theme have consistently been sounded in DES publications. *The Education of Immigrants*[35] referred to language teaching as "the most urgent single challenge facing the schools." In *The Continuing Needs of Immigrants*,[36] DES urged that attention be paid to language difficulties persisting even after the rudiments of English had been acquired. Within H.M. inspectorate, an independent institution working with DES and intimately involved with local authorities, the small unit concerned with racial policy has also stressed the importance of language instruction.

As DES well knew, merely to call for instruction in English without providing more tangible help would have been an empty gesture, for local authorities lacked the teachers and the money adequately to do the job. The government did indeed do more.[37] In 1965, authorities with a sizable immigrant student population were permitted to hire teachers in excess of the then existing ceiling—with their own resources. The Local Government Act, passed the following year, offered financial support—50, later 75 percent of teaching staff salaries—to aid authorities in coping with "the presence within their areas of substantial numbers of immigrants from the Commonwealth whose language or customs differ from those of the community." Some 12 million pounds were spent on that program in 1975. A nationally supported curriculum project produced needed materials for teaching the non-English speaking, particularly at the primary school level. Efforts were made in teachers' colleges and, subsequently, in in-service programs, to give teachers the language teaching skills needed to cope with the demands of this group. Most recently, the government has funded "industrial language centres," which teach English to immigrants working in factories or preparing for such work.

With respect to language acquisition, the obvious became policy: every British child was to be rendered at least minimally competent in English. Generating shared acceptance for that goal and encouraging its realization are not trivial accomplishments, as the troubled history of bilingual education in the United States reveals. Consistent with the strongly localist education tradition, the implementation of this policy has been left to local education authorities. For that reason, the national commitment has assumed different meanings from place to place.[38] A few authorities identified those needing special help by passing every Asian immigrant child through a "reception center"; the more typical pattern was to rely on teachers' classroom assessments of language difficulties, as these became apparent. Arrangements for instruction also varied markedly. At one extreme, full-time language centers introduced immigrants to basic English, sometimes interlaced with a kind of cultural orientation. At the other extreme, authorities either made no special efforts—a not uncommon practice at the elementary age level—or deployed the services of peripatetic teachers who offered language instruction for only an hour or two each week.

There has been no visible effort by DES to impose its preference for language instruction on local authorities: this too is generally consistent with DES policy. As a result of the *laissez faire* policy, there remain profound variations in both program content and local support, as reflected in the amount of Local Government Act moneys requested by different communities.[39] Harrow and Derby, for instance, each enroll about 8,000 pupils classified as "New Commonwealth Immigrants" (NCI); in 1975, the former secured less than 50 pence of Local Government Act money for each nonwhite child, the latter more than 25 pounds per child, 50 times as much. Nor is this the rare case. Authorities enrolling only about one-third of all NCIs claimed more than half of the Local Government Act funds.[40]

This variability is partly a matter of ideology. In 1970, educators could still defend the modesty of their language teaching efforts as deriving from a desire "not to draw attention to the immigrant community" or as premised on a "reluctance to make provision for immigrant pupils which was not equally available to non-immigrant pupils."[41] Such authorities were, however, decidedly the exception. In the main, communities which spent little on language teaching did so not out of principle but rather because of a perceived lack of resources. They were only too willing to urge upon DES sizable new nationally funded undertakings.[42]

This shared enthusiasm for treating the problem in terms of language is easily understood. An inability to speak English is one distinguishing characteristic that an educational system cannot ignore: it is important both of itself and in its impact on intellectual comprehension generally. Further, language instruction is a concrete pedagogical task, one well within the competence of the school. If teaching English to Punjabi-speaking youngsters is not quite like teaching English children French, neither is it so terribly different. Language teaching is also an enterprise in which definite progress could be marked, competency noted; the task has none of the quicksand characteristics of institutional concern for human, or community, relations.

The language problems of nonwhite students are, of course, real enough. Yet these factors make language such an attractive focus that they encourage DES to define the educational problem in terms of language even when these do not well fit the case at hand. West Indian educational problems afford an apt illustration. When in the early 1970s the previously little-noticed school difficulties of West Indians came to light, the strong temptation was for DES to perceive the West Indians as afflicted with language problems akin to those that had more obviously beset Pakistani and Indian students. Yet by this time the Creole dialect, the ostensible cause of the West Indians' schooling problems, was, according to a report of the Community Relations Commission, no longer being spoken as a primary language by the British West Indians.[43]

While nonwhites as newcomers were also unfamiliar with the culture and customs of Britain, the development of an appropriate policy response in this domain proved more problematic than assaults on language deficiencies. The initial aspiration of the government was straightforward: render the newcomers at ease with their surroundings by making them over into Britons. The task of the education system, then, was to inculcate British values—whatever those might be. As the Commonwealth Immigrants Advisory Council argued in 1964:

> A national system of education must aim at producing citizens who can take their place in society properly equipped to exercise rights and perform duties

> the same as those of other citizens. If their parents were brought up in another culture and another tradition, children should be encouraged to respect it, but a national system cannot be expected to perpetuate the different values of immigrant children.[44]

DES described the educational task as involving the "successful assimiliation of immigrant children," an enterprise dependent "on a realistic understanding of the adjustments that they have to make."[45] The adjustment of the British school was apparently a matter of hearing out the immigrants when the lessons included matters "concerned with their own countries."

The effort to disperse nonwhite students, encouraged by DES in the mid-1960s, was at least partly motivated by the desire to achieve cultural assimilation. A racially identifiable group would be distributed among the population. Living in a predominantly English-speaking environment, it would come naturally to speak that language. Dominated by British ways, its members would come to make these its own.

The rhetoric of assimilation was ultimately too inconsistent with presumed British tolerance of diversity, and too unpalatable to nonwhites, to endure—at least as official policy. In 1966, Roy Jenkins, the Home Secretary, announced a different aspiration. The national goal was "not a flattening process of assimilation but an equal opportunity accompanied by cultural diversity, in an atmosphere of mutual tolerance."[46] This rhetoric was as irresistible as it was vague. It became the watchword in DES, where it was linked with the obfuscations of multiculturalism. By 1971, in *The Education of Immigrants,* DES was claiming:

> Schools can demonstrate how people from different ethnic groups and cultural backgrounds can live together happily and successfully, and can help to create the kind of cohesive, multi-cultural society on

> which the future of this country—and possibly the world—depends.[47]

A few years later, the parliamentary Select Committee on Race Relations and Immigration called for "unity through diversity"[48] in the schools. At the rhetorical level, there existed official consensus on a position consistent with that advanced by nonwhite leaders such as Jeff Crawford, president of the Caribbean Teachers' Association:

> The British school is now a multi-colored leopard, substantially white but with specks of brown and black. . . . Therefore the schools have got to cater increasingly to the various cultures which exist in the schools. . . .[49]

Self-reports from the education authorities revealed that local practice had changed less than national rhetoric. The locals' concerns, if exotic in nature, were more matters of style than substance. While the presence of nonwhites tested the schools' commitment to a particular British conformity, it did not otherwise penetrate deeply into the life of the schools.[50] "Moslems refuse to uncover their legs—especially girls"; "Asian girls will not take part in country dancing unless the class is single sex"; "a Sikh may wear a turban and is indeed encouraged to do so as his hair becomes unmanageably long and has to be plaited. He may also wear the ceremonial shorts, comb and bangle, but *not* the dagger!" That last school was liberal-minded, as British schools went. Others insisted that turbans be abandoned, and would not accept appropriately colored shalwars (pants) as a substitute for the school uniform skirt.

Minimal recognition of cultural differences was one thing, more basic alteration of the character of the institution something else again.[51] One radical commentator imagined minority students using their uniqueness as an ideological weapon—"if a large number of youth in a school speak only Punjabi or Gujarati, it becomes impossible to grade them . . ."[52]—but there were few in the nonwhite community who entertained such fantasies. For its part, DES did not regard cultural heterogeneity as an educational asset. Quite the contrary:

> So many immigrant children . . . so often do not find the required intellectual stimulus [in their homes] that there is little cause for surprise that not only the intellectual performance but also the intellectual status of so many of these children is depressed.[53]

The possibility that the schools offer native language instruction was resisted by DES, which asserted that such a venture was inconsistent with its concern for integration. Local authorities were equally unenthusiastic. "The community relations officer thinks we should be teaching Gujarati, but we couldn't start that caper."[54] Black studies proposals received a similarly cool reception.[55] Multiculturalism was apparently to be confined to the symbolic gesture, the ceremonial shorts worn without the dagger. To do otherwise risked catering to intellectual weakness, as well as promoting social divisiveness.

Language and cultural differences, as DES viewed these concepts, betokened an educational problem of limited duration. As the newcomers became familiar with British ways, their difficulties would diminish. To some extent, this hope has been borne out in practice. With the imposition of ever tighter immigration restrictions, the absolute number of newcomers has declined drastically: about two out of every three nonwhite schoolchildren are now British-born. Because of this change in the composition of the nonwhite population, language deficiencies have assumed less significance. Between 1967 and 1970, the proportion of NCI children reported by their teachers as experiencing language difficulties dropped from one in four to one in six.[56] Nonwhites whose entire education had taken place in Britain performed markedly better than more recent arrivals, although by no means as well as the indigenous population. In mathematics, for example, 11.7 percent of the wholly English-educated nonwhites were in the top quartile of mathematics performance, as compared with just 6 percent of the newer arrivals.[57]

The perception that nonwhites have serious educational problems has not correspondingly diminished—particularly in the minority communities, which have demanded that attention be paid to their special needs. Among West Indians, concern over poor academic achievement has increasingly been voiced; attention has been drawn to the long-existing West Indian communities in Liverpool and Cardiff where nonwhite academic performance has remained depressed for several generations.[58] More generally, the belief that the educational problem was merely transitional and would be resolved naturally is now regarded as overly optimistic. As the National Association of Schoolmasters observed:

> It was hoped that, given goodwill, perceptible advances could be made in the relatively short term towards the integration of the white and coloured peoples. Further experience serves to show that integration is more difficult to achieve than was hoped.[59]

By the late 1960s, nonwhites were no longer newcomers, and had to be described in other terms. Again, the terms chosen were pointedly not racial. Stress came to be laid first on urban deprivation, then on educational disadvantage. Both categories engulfed minority inner city children in the vastly larger population of lower class urban whites, rather than pinpointing concern on their particular plight.

The government's preference for redressing broad categories of social need, instead of responding to the particular grievances of groups such as nonwhites, was reflected in the 1968 Urban Programme.[60] Under that program, support for a variety of public services including education is made available to authorities "required . . . to incur expenditure by reason . . . of special social need." The initial expectation was that the Urban Programme would expand upon the Local Government Act initiative, and would be available exclusively to communities with high concentrations of nonwhites. This has not been the case. As government circulars have pointed out, "the Urban Programme should not be thought of as an immigrants' programme, but a programme mainly concerned with urban need wherever, and in whatever form it exists."[61]

If the presence of racial minorities is not irrelevant to this concept of policy desert, neither is it central. Despite a "gentlemen's agreement" to pay particular heed to the needs of communities whose problems stemmed from the presence of nonwhites,[62] only an estimated 10 percent of Urban Programme money has actually been so expended.[63] And at least in the Urban Programme's first phases, expenditure categories responded to general societal needs—nursery school programs, for instance—rather than to specifically minority concerns.

In 1973, the Select Committee on Race Relations and Immigration, concluding its assessment of education policy, called for a government program particularly focused on race. A fund for "the special educational needs of immigrant children," administered by DES, to which local authorities would apply, should be created, the committee asserted.[64] Although the committee spoke of "immigrants," not racial minorities, it was clear from the hearings that race, rather than newness or language difficulties, lay behind this suggestion. As one committee member had noted: "I am going to call immigrant children coloured children, because these are the children we are talking about here." Throughout the committee hearings, "coloured" rather than "immigrant" was the common term of reference and the common source of concern.

In this context, "immigrant" is a legislative term of art, a euphemism for nonwhite.

Had the committee's proposal received DES support, the consequences would have been noteworthy. For one thing, the presence of new money would likely have generated a demand to influence its expenditure among minority groups as well as local authorities, thus spurring political efforts among nonwhites. For another, as manager of these funds, DES would have been obliged to develop race-specific policies.[65] DES, however, would have none of it. The department's published reply, *Educational Disadvantage and the Educational Needs of Immigrants,*[66] lambasted the proposal. DES recognized that "many of those born here, of all ethnic minority groups, will experience continuing difficulties, which must receive special attention from the education service." But no new program was needed to assure this special attention. All those who suffer educational disadvantage, whatever their race, have common needs. Nonwhites are not different in this regard, and would accordingly "benefit increasingly from special help given to all those suffering from educational disadvantage." Race was too explosive and too educationally unproductive a category to warrant specific attention.

The institutional response was consistent with this analysis. DES created a small unit concerned with educational disadvantage within the department, and an independent Centre for Advice and Information on Educational Disadvantage, budgeted at 180,000 pounds per year. Within both organizations, nonwhites would have to jockey for attention with all the other claimants to the mantle of disadvantage, among them the London Cockney and the fabled Irish gypsy. By all reports, they have not done particularly well in that affray.[67]

DES has consistently preferred almost any identifying label—"non-English speaking," "culturally deprived," "educationally disadvantaged"—to the racial one. The department maintained this position when, during the 1972 hearings of the Select Committee on Race Relations and Immigration, West Indians voiced unhappiness with the fact that their children were disproportionately represented in classes for the educationally subnormal. DES was, at the time, willing only to consider consulting about the matter with local authorities; to do more would presumably have constituted interference with longstanding traditions of local autonomy. Four years later, a question posed at a hearing held by the same parliamentary committee revealed that nothing had resulted from the consultations. Indeed, DES did not know whether the over-representation persisted.

Even more illuminating was the fate of DES-maintained statistics on race. Beginning in 1966, DES asked local authorities to estimate the number of NCI children either born in Commonwealth countries other than Canada, Australia, and New Zealand or born of parents who had emigrated from those countries to Britain within the past ten years. This category, used to allocate Local Government Act money, combines a concern for newcomers with a veiled interest in race, for immigrants from the New Commonwealth are almost exclusively nonwhite. The category offended some, who viewed this statistic keeping as a racial insult. It more generally irked educators who saw no educational purpose to be served by this definition of "immigrant," since no educational need was spelled out.

DES's response to these criticisms was to abolish the statistics entirely. At the 1973 Select Committee hearings on education, Margaret Thatcher, then Minister for Education and Science, observed: "My Department makes no use of them whatsoever except to publish them. They do not form the basis of any grant from my Department . . . none of our grant formulae are on the basis of immigrants."[68]

Technically, Mrs. Thatcher was correct: while the NCI statistics were used to distribute Local Government Act money, the Home Office and not DES was formally responsible for that program. The impact of DES's actions was, however, significant. From one point of view, the NCI statistics permitted quantification of what could be described as a "problem." One knew from them how many "immigrant"—and in almost all cases nonwhite—children were to be found in particular authorities; one could, through administration of examinations, determine the educational progress of these students; one might even design programs with this group especially in mind. The simple expedient of no longer having a statistically identified group about which to talk had the undeniable effect of making it harder to focus attention on that group's particular needs.

A more positive view of DES's decision may also be maintained. In 1972, no one knew what a beneficial race-specific program should look like (the same is true today, for that matter). There was also strong principled opposition to relying on racial identification for any reason; on this point, the lesson of the American experience was mixed. The DES action conceivably helped to avert or at least postpone an overtly racial battle over the ends of schooling. That is just the kind of goal that racial inexplicitness is supposed to achieve: it represents doing good by doing little.

The Sources of Racial Inexplicitness

Inexplicitness with respect to the racial aspects of educational policy, which characterizes the British experience, did not arise by happenstance. It is consistent with a pronounced political and bureaucratic preference for consensual, incremental decision making, a preference threatened by the confrontationist, potentially revolutionary nature of a racial orientation. It is also traceable to a deep-seated ideological commitment to universalism in social services, and a consequent allergy to group labelling for even purportedly benign governmental purposes.

These complementary phenomena have encouraged DES to leave race alone where possible, and also to adopt policies which render nonwhites better off insofar as they help everyone, or at least everyone in need, rather than specially benefiting nonwhites. Such an approach has been presumed likely to achieve more for racial minorities in the long run, and with rather less social pain, than the alternative of a more overtly racial focus.

Consensual Decision Making. When confronted by demands that it undertake almost anything, the prototypical DES response is to stress its own institutional powerlessness. At one level, this departmental modesty fairly reflects the facts. While the power formally assigned to the Secretary of State for DES by the 1944 Educational Act sounds formidable—"to secure the effective utilization by local education authorities under his control and direction, of a national policy for providing a varied and comprehensive educational service in every area; [to prevent] any local education authority . . . [from] act[ing] or proposing to act unreasonably"—the reality is considerably less prepossessing.

The statutory provision permitting the Secretary of State to overturn "unreasonable" local authority actions was thought to grant essentially unlimited discretion. A 1976 decision of the House of Lords, however, read this grant of power narrowly: only if no reasonable local authority could have reached a particular decision is the Secretary of State justified in intervening.[69] This court decision arose in the context of a challenge to DES's demand that all authorities shift to comprehensive secondary schools, undoubtedly the major educational policy initiative of the past 15 years. The judicial setback to that effort, even though quickly overcome by positive legislation, doubtless diminished the department's desire further to test the scope of its broad legal mandate. The more specific powers granted by the 1944 act are, in the main, "limited, mostly financial and negative."[70] At least until very recently, direction giving with respect to race has not been among these specific mandates.[71]

By itself, lack of authority does not explain DES's tendency not to intervene in a great many educational matters. The department could, after all, seek further powers by proposing new legislation; and the example of continental European systems, where substantially more authority lodges in the central educational administration, is familiar. But more power, in the formal sense, is apparently not wanted. The British educational system is conventionally described as a partnership of national government and local authorities. The complex web of interrelationships—not only among government entities but also among teachers' and headmasters' and parents' groups, research and exam-writing organizations, numerous special interest organizations, and the like—betokens a form of governance more subtle than partnership. The Permanent Secretary of DES did not exaggerate when declaring: "Consultation is a way of life with us."[72]

In such a "pluralistic, incremental, unsystematic, reactive"[73] system, formal power counts for less than informal suasion. Bold initiatives are far less common than nuanced pressures on local authorities—through the inspectorate, for instance, which assesses their instructional offerings. Occasions when a policy change—such as adopting the comprehensive structure—is required, not merely recommended, are rare. In a ministry described by the Organization for Economic Cooperation and Development (OECD) as "pragmatic, conservative and evolutionary, not theoretical, futurologic, and revolutionary,"[74] few rules will be issued, except after the achievement of consensus. This is so not only because the department's formal rule-making powers are bounded, a fact that became fully evident only in 1976, but because rule making intended to alter local authority behavior is uncongenial.

In such an environment, there are few worse failings than to attempt leadership, only to discover an absence of followers. That was the fate of the 1965 DES circular recommending that authorities disperse, or bus, in order to break up concentrations of immigrant students. Many authorities, among them those with the greatest number of nonwhite students, either ignored or publicly opposed the suggestion. Circulars are supposed to have received general approval from the interested and politically significant parties before being issued; that this one hadn't was painfully evident. The denouement of the dispersal issue, a gradual DES retreat from its busing recommendation, was not one which the department might be thought eager to repeat. It may well have promoted departmental caution with respect to race more generally.

DES's negative response to the Select Committee recommendation that the department allocate money specifically for immigrant education programs and monitor local authority efforts was also consistent with its apparent lack of taste for directive behavior. The proposal, DES declared, presumes:

> that local education authorities will not take initiatives to improve the education of immigrants unless there is an earmarked Department of Education and Science fund on which they can draw to meet the cost. . . . The Government do not believe that [this] argument is borne out by experience.[75]

Decisions concerning the wise expenditure of limited education resources, DES added, are properly made by local authorities. "If specific grants for particular aspects of education in which the local authorities have previously enjoyed discretion were to be introduced, the effect might be to reduce the scope of local responsibility."

Perhaps DES was merely disclaiming any interest in bureaucratic expansionism. Or perhaps, in the midst of the struggle over comprehensive schooling, this was not an issue over which the department wished to brook another test of its powers, recognizing the manifest lack of consensus for any course of action. Whatever the precise reason, the institutionally rooted preference for deference to local authorities effectively limited race-specific policy initiatives.

A desire within DES for consensus concerning the substance of policies has been matched by a desire to minimize conflict in the negotiation of policies. That fact too has had a bearing on DES reluctance to address race-specific issues; OECD summarized the department's position on the matter:

> When it comes to planning leading to policy decisions . . . informal methods, utilized by sensitive and fair-minded government servants, are superior to highly structured formal procedures which invite half-baked and politically sectarian battles, and encourage demagogy, confrontation, and publicity. . . .[76]

DES places decided limits on the consultative enterprise, and these would naturally have tended to exclude race as a topic of widespread consultation. From the department's point of view, attending to race might have been calculated to produce bile, not balm. To note just one difficulty: How would DES determine which racial groups to consult, without arousing controversy in the process? If the education committee of the communist Indian Workers' Association was to be called upon, what about the education committee of the fascist National Front? Better, the department might well have concluded, not to make the effort at all. At any event, the documented failure to consult minority groups—even with respect to such obvious occasions for consultation as in responding to the call for native language teaching pressed by the European Economic Community—undoubtedly contributed to a lack of any substantive focus on race.

Universalism. Structural constraints and decision-making style only partially explain DES resistance to a race-specific focus. One needs also to understand the universalist ideology on which the provision of social services in Britain has been broadly premised for the past three decades, and the tension between race specificity and universalism.

Central to what has been termed the postwar British revolution in social welfare policy is an ideological commitment to the universal provision of social services, rather than a selective distribution on the basis of a showing of individual indigency.[77] To have to prove oneself poor or otherwise deserving before receiving schooling or medical attention is condemned on several grounds. Insofar as the selective criterion forced individuals to demean themselves in order to obtain help, it imposes a stigma. Over time, that societal stigma is thought to evolve into self-stigmatization as the needy come, because of this circumstance, to think less well of themselves. "If men are treated as a burden to others . . . then, in time they will behave as a burden."[78] Selective efforts also equate need with fault, ignoring the structural elements of modern economies that render such blaming wholly unconvincing. Moreover, selectivity creates invidious differentiations with respect to the service offered—what the poor get will be worse than what is available to the better off—and so divides the society.

A universalist approach, by contrast, in which an individual's entitlement to social service has no relationship to social status, is held to foster a badly needed sense of community, discouraging traditional class and status antagonisms. "It is not (or should be)," argued Richard Titmuss, the most passionate postwar advocate of universalism, "an objective of social policy to build the identity of a person around some community with which he is associated."[79] While universalism addresses itself particularly to social class-based differentiation, this generating of national community through status-blind treatment is also thought a particularly appropriate way of drawing racial minorities into the larger society.[80]

By comparison with prewar Britain, basic individual needs—in education, health care, and social security particularly—are now far more equally met. Need itself counts for more, social status for less, than before. Not that universalism by itself ever has been or could be the basis for coherent policy: it is more a slogan, the banner for an exuberantly romantic socialism, than social reality. As long as individual demands are greater than the collective willingness to share resources, some selectivity is required; for that reason, the universalist is "driven reluctantly towards stringency in allocation."[81] Nor do the universalists forget that certain social categories broadly deserve to benefit from "positive discrimination"; to ignore poverty, for instance, is only to transmit inequity by producing that mythical equality of the stork and the fox. Titmuss himself is clear on this point: "To me, the 'Welfare State' has no meaning unless it is positively and constructively concerned with redistributive justice. . . ."[82] Yet the question remains: How can the government prefer some (and which categories of "some"?), even as it serves all?

Positive discrimination is, then, a most problematic concept for the universalist. As Richard Titmuss has framed the issue:

> The challenge that faces us is not the choice between universalist and selective social services. The real

> challenge resides in the question: what particular infrastructure of universalist services is needed in order to provide a framework of values and opportunity within and around which can be developed socially acceptable selective services aiming to discriminate positively, with the minimum risk of stigma, in favour of those whose needs are greatest.[83]

Selectivity is essential, but selectivity has to be both as little noticed amid the general welfare system and as psychologically undemeaning as possible. These concerns have prompted the policy suggestion that positive discrimination "should not be confined to particular individuals and families but must help everyone in the chosen area";[84] in that way, the "deserving" social group member does not have to identify himself as such. Similarly, in education stress has been placed on providing resources for education priority areas, rather than on aiding particular types of individuals.[85] Although these efforts do not eliminate stigma—the "area" approach may merely transfer stigma from the class of persons to the place[86]—the desire to reduce stigma has animated such undertakings.

Positive discrimination presents another related puzzle: Can it be practiced in a way that does not arouse the resentment of the nonbeneficiaries? If not, the consensual framework on which universalist policy rests, the nationally shared acceptance of the "need to diminish both the absolute fact and the psychological sense of social and economic discrimination,"[87] will collapse. Without such a consensus, the policy is, in Titmuss's terms, no longer "socially acceptable."

To the universalist, a race-specific educational policy properly raises all of these concerns. Special attention would predictably arouse antagonisms, not private consensus, for there is little shared sense that nonwhites are more deserving than, say, the poor generally. "Why them and not us?" remains the likely white reaction. For this reason, local authorities have often been willing to aid nonwhites only at moments when white residents were, so to speak, looking the other way. Nor is stigmatization easily avoided; aiding racial minorities might just reinforce the long-standing British impression that these groups are, after all, inferior.[88]

Even if the policy maker overcomes these obstacles, there remains a vital further problem: the dimensions of a positive, race-specific policy are hardly clear. The Community Relations Commission could call upon DES to produce a "clear and unequivocal policy" concerning race;[89] it stumbled only when it had to give substance to the suggestion. There thus exists the very real possibility that any race-specific approach would be of little use to the very group it is intended to benefit. Far better, or so it may be argued, to define educational needs in terms of language or culture, tangible concerns to which no blame could attach. Better also to stress, as DES did, the shared "educational disadvantages associated with an impoverished environment,"[90] in the expectation that the benefits flowing to that large and amorphous group would simultaneously be felt by the smaller, more visible, more vulnerable racial minority. Given such a view of the world, one helps nonwhites by *not* favoring them explicitly. The benefits to minorities from such an approach are thought to be real if invisible—or better, real because invisible. If race is officially ignored, even against the weight of the evidence, its relevance might just disappear over time.

The ideological preference for universalism, which finds more mundane expression as unhappiness with "special treatment" or "favoritism," has been conjoined with a style and structure of decision making resistant to definitive policy making of any sort. Arrayed against these, the bases for a race-specific policy appear, on close inspection, quite weak. In Britain, the minority population has never been able to coalesce into a community; it remains fragmented and innocent of the political arts.[91] The race relations cottage industry, functioning both inside and outside of government, has not been taken particularly seriously by DES. Moreover, as the parliamentary Select Committee on Race Relations and Immigration noted in 1974, the two government-created agencies, the Community Relations Commission and the Race Relations Board, have failed "to make sufficient impact or to gain the confidence of the ethnic communities."[92] Because the nongovernmental groups' energies have been committed to battling against increasingly restrictive immigration laws, it has been difficult, as a practical matter, for them to argue simultaneously for liberalized immigration—in part on the grounds that immigration is not problem creating—and for attending to the problems associated with race.[93] The academic community has had little of policy relevance to offer, and what it has contributed has tended to downplay the importance of race.[94] There thus has been no effective counterforce to the racially inexplicit policies consistently pursued by DES.

Inexplicitness, Race, and Schooling

In several related ways, DES has pursued a policy of inexplicitness with respect to issues of race and schooling. DES has consistently defined educational problems posed by the nonwhite presence in nonracial terms: as reflecting language difficulties or lack of cultural familiarity, or as an indistinguishable aspect of the dilemmas associated with educational disadvantage generally. Challenges to that policy—the insistence that race-specific measures be attempted, especially on behalf of West Indian schoolchildren—have been rebuffed by DES, which has been unwilling even to maintain a count of nonwhites in British schools.

Just what is one to make of British race and schooling policy? A decade ago, Richard Titmuss chided America for not adopting a universalist approach:

> The American failure has been due to the belief that poverty was the problem and that [within the context of poverty] the advance of the poor Negro could be presented as a pro-Negro enterprise. This has not been seen as a universalist problem of inequality, social justice, exclusion.[95]

Turnabout is fair play: or so the American ambassador to the United Nations, Andrew Young, presumably thought when, flipping Titmuss's argument on its head, he criticized Britain as "a little bit chicken" on matters of race.[96] For their part, the British, who used to discern the virtues of their own approach to race by contrasting Britain's relative tranquillity with the plagues that beset the American house, are no longer so convinced of their own rightness. A parade of critics has chided the government in general, and DES in particular, for its inattentiveness to nonwhite concerns. The parliamentary Select Committee on Race Relations and Immigration scored DES for its haphazard responses to the issue; the Community Relations Commission and the privately financed Runnymede Trust have used harsher language in conveying the same point of view.

While it may be in the nature of things for organizations concerned primarily with race policy never to feel that their constituents are treated well enough, something more than interest group politics is going on here. In an open letter to the Secretary of State for DES, Peter Walker, the Conservative M.P., noted the department's "remarkable complacency" with respect to racial issues. The Labour Party's Home Policy Committee has weighed in with an assault on "long periods of [DES] inaction punctuated by hasty and inadequate measures" concerning race.[97]

These arguments are not new, but only now do they appear to be having some effect. The 1976 Race Relations Act specifies that discrimination with respect to education is unlawful; the predecessor act spoke only of discrimination with respect to services generally. The new act also empowers DES to review local education authority behavior and to consider individual claims of discrimination before these are brought to court. These provisions oblige DES to develop some policy, at least with respect to discrimination questions, if not the broader problems of race. For another, immediately following the publication in 1977 of the Select Committee's Report on the West Indian community, DES indicated its willingness to undertake an inquiry into the specific causes of West Indian underachievement in British schools.[98] Where research goes, demands for further governmental attention—most likely, for money on the heads of nonwhite students—are sure to follow. The result is likely to be a more direct DES involvement with race than has thus far been the case. Is this a sensible policy course?

Providing benefits to the poor without stigma constituted a vital social policy problem for postwar Britain. Adding a racial element only complicates the task. As Titmuss ruefully noted: "Redistribution is now inextricably mixed up with the challenge of social rights as well as civil rights for 'coloured' citizens."[99] From the viewpoint of the critics, the British response has failed on two counts. It has not involved racial minorities, as communities, in the process of determining their own fate. It has also provided meagre substantive "benefits" for the nonwhite community.

In all the discussions over the proper place of race in educational policy, nonwhite voices have seldom been heard. The government undertook to act in the best interests of a silent constituency. It acted for the racial minorities rather than with them, and in that sense was truly paternalistic. Neither universalism, the broad policy objective, nor consensualism, the preferred style, were inventions of the minority communities.

Because there was no "nonwhite community," at least in the political sense, it may be argued that decisions had to be made on its behalf. That response is not necessarily persuasive. A study of the collapse of one civil rights group, the Committee Against Racial Discrimination, in the late 1960s, concludes:

> Given a broad definition of social rights that includes some concept of cultural diversity, the attempt by government to guarantee social rights for all citizens—regardless of race—may require more than a redistribution of social benefits; it may also require a redistribution of power, through which groups of immigrants can participate as political equals in a collectivist, pluralist political system. . . . The challenge to government is to share power as a means of developing the organizations or institutions for immigrants and their children.[100]

Concern about participatory values might matter less had the minority community benefited tangibly, in substantive terms, from the policy of racial inexplicitness. Inexplicitness might, in other words, be viewed not as betokening policy neglect, but rather as doing good by stealth, involving quiet good works which could not have been undertaken explicitly. If one takes spending as an empirical measure of benefit, this does not appear to have been the case.[101] In 1975–76, central government expenditure for private and secondary education (excluding special programs and school meals) totalled a bit more than 3 billion pounds. Some 12,215,000 pounds, four-tenths of 1 percent of the education budget, were used to subsidize teachers' salaries in communities with substantial immigrant concentrations under Local Government Act. An estimated 10 percent of the 10,022,000 pounds of

Urban Programme moneys spent on education went to local authority activities in which minorities were significant participants. If one makes the too generous assumption that all Local Government Act and Urban Programme moneys actually were spent on nonwhites, each nonwhite child received a supplementary benefit of less than 40 pounds; in fact, since Local Government Act moneys are effectively general aid for the eligible authorities, the true figure would be substantially lower.

The former DES secretary, Sir Edward Boyle (now Lord Boyle), once noted that, as concerns race and education, British policy makers vacillate between the illusion of competence and "talking themselves into a quite unnecessary crisis."[102] The assault on inexplicitness falls into the latter category. If inexplicitness has not been so clearly right as its defenders have asserted, neither has it been so misguided as critics would have it. It may be best appreciated as one plausible approach to a set of immensely troubling issues.

Consider the actual policy problems that have confronted DES. As concerns the participation issue, in the absence of sustained minority community pressure what would it have meant for government to "share power"? Was DES properly expected to invent a minority leadership? To put the question differently, Was there really an alternative to paternalism? For DES to undertake a "redistribution of power" bespeaks substantive as well as processual change of most uncertain consequence. With respect to substantive matters, is it clear that a program directed particularly at minority underachievement (or minority educational *anomie*) would have done much good? Might it merely have inflated expectations without affecting educational outcomes? Would Britain's racial minorities have been better served by the British equivalent to Title I of the 1965 Elementary and Secondary Education Act, an American compensatory education program in which bookkeeping concerns—are only eligible children benefiting?—have too often driven out educational concerns—is *anyone* benefiting?

DES's position on these immensely complex and troubling matters is presently in a state of flux. Its most recent report, *The West Indian Community: Observations on the Report of the Select Committee*,[103] alters departmental policy in several significant ways. The report itself was preceded by consultations with some fifty West Indian organizations who had expressed interest in the issue; in that sense, DES adopted a less paternalistic mode of decision making than it has in the past. The substance of this document also differs from earlier forays. DES is now willing to undertake an inquiry concerning the academic performance of ethnic minorities (Asians and Africans as well as West Indians); to collect data concerning nonwhite students, which will permit a review of the extent of nonwhite overrepresentation in classes for the educationally subnormal; and to step up recruitment of nonwhite teachers. Each of these efforts is likely to increase race-consciousness in schooling policy.

With respect to providing special funding for nonwhite students, DES—and, subsequently, the Home Office—drew the line. While the Urban Programme, whose funds benefit authorities in which nonwhites disproportionately reside, has been quadrupled in size, the government remains unwilling to earmark funds especially for nonwhites. For its part, the Home Office proposed substantial changes in Section 11 of the 1966 Local Government Act, the present source of much special funding, consistent with the DES view.[104] If the changes are accepted by Parliament, Section 11 funds will be available, not just for adding staff, but also "to alleviate any special features of social and educational disadvantage suffered by these groups" and "to promote equal educational opportunity and good relations between such groups and the general population." This greater breadth of permissible purpose, coupled with expansion of the population whose needs may be served by the programs as well as a requirement that educational authorities solicit (rather than being automatically entitled to) funds, should permit energetic authorities to attempt innovative ventures that, in their judgment, will help to alleviate the difficulties that nonwhites have encountered. Inexplicitness remains the policy norm. As *The West Indian Community* report declared: "As the most fundamental needs of the ethnic minorities are essentially the same as those of the population as a whole, it is through the general expenditure programmes . . . that these needs should be met. The general programmes need however to adapt themselves to the presence of the ethnic minorities. . . ."

These reforms attempt a middle course between a policy of deliberate inattention, on the one hand, and an elaborate and explicitly racial undertaking, on the other. They offer no panaceas: But what alternative does? At the end of a systematic assessment of discrimination and racial disadvantage in Britain, David Smith offers a warning: "If the children . . . find that the educational system has passed them by . . . then there will be the profound frustration, bitterness, and disorientation that is already seen in young West Indians. . . ."[105] The point is well taken, and sobering for a nation just beginning to peer behind the camouflage of tolerance at its social reality. But the critical question remains: What other educational policy might Britain have pursued, with any assurance that the nation's racial dilemmas would thereby have been eased? Only the ideologue who lacks an appreciation for the ironies of social history could offer a confident reply.

three

Busing and (Liberal) Backlash in Britain

The Vagaries of Busing Policy

In 1963, the outer London borough of Southall became the first British community to bus, or disperse, nonwhite students.[1] Several hundred nonwhites were sent from schools whose composition had within the preceding five years become predominantly nonwhite and poor to schools that were primarily white and middle class. This practice was continued and expanded when Southall merged with neighboring Ealing: in time, as many as 3,000 youngsters rode the buses each day.

Ealing was a pioneer of sorts in race policy. Its dispersal efforts received explicit approval from the DES, which formally urged that other communities with sizable ethnic minority concentrations do likewise. During the mid-1960s, dispersal was endorsed by both the Conservative and Labour parties; insofar as liberal spokesmen of all races addressed the matter, it commanded their support as well. Years before busing became a scare-word in the American political lexicon, the practice was in place and functioning tolerably well in several English cities.

Fifteen years later, Ealing found itself defending its dispersal policy in the British courts against the claim that busing is discriminatory, and ultimately announcing its intention to abandon that policy in the face of the legal assault.[2] This very circumstance is noteworthy. More striking yet, the lawsuit was not initiated by a disgruntled parent. No identifiable individual claiming to be hurt by busing participated in the litigation. The plaintiff in the case was instead the Race Relations Board, an institution which, to judge from its views on race, might well have praised and not condemned this venture. How is this apparent reversal of national policy, culminating in the adoption of a position seemingly at odds with the American legal understanding of discrimination, to be explained?

The evolution of busing policy in Britain has received nearly no attention. This disinterest is, in one respect, readily understandable. Only a tiny minority of British nonwhites has ever been bused. The proportion of nonwhites remains, at 4 percent, relatively small, and, of these, a goodly number is "naturally" dispersed. In 1970, the last time school-by-school data were collected, only 569 out of Britain's 26,000 schools enrolled more than one-third nonwhite children;[3] among the rest, the issue of dispersal generally did not arise. For both ideological and political reasons, the education authorities with the greatest numbers and proportions of minority students engaged in no busing.

Moreover, busing never became as politically volatile in Britain as in America. Neither the British courts nor DES ever imposed busing on a community. Adoption or rejection of dispersal has been in each instance a local decision, one premised exclusively on political and pedagogical considerations. Partly for this reason, busing provoked little reported resistance among whites into whose schools nonwhites were bused: the decision was, in a very real sense, theirs to make.[4] Precisely because busing was essentially a white-initiated policy, one whose motivating impulses were decidedly mixed, it aroused little excitement among racial minorities, who were in any event too fragmented and politically weak to exercise much influence over policy. Busing in Britain is, in short, almost a non-issue.

Almost, but not quite: as the incidents in Ealing suggest, dispersal may usefully be examined on several distinct levels. The ins and outs of policy, including a recounting of the tensions among agencies within the national government and between national and local government, make for a rich tale. The busing history also offers a useful lens through which to view British attitudes toward race and schooling. Busing is necessarily racially explicit. In this sense, it is decidedly the deviant policy case in Britain, where educational policy has otherwise consistently sought to avoid attending to the phenomenon of race. The ultimate abandonment of busing by DES draws attention to this norm of inexplicitness, an ideologically and politically rooted reluctance to single out nonwhites for any purpose, whether allegedly benevolent or malign.

In yet another respect, dispersal represents an important exception to the norms of educational policy making. The process by which policy is shaped in Britain is quintessentially political, informed by ideology and by educational wisdom according to the politicians' and bureaucrats' taste. It is not a matter for the courts: the British judiciary, quite unlike its American counterpart, has had scarcely any say in educational policy matters.[5] The 1976 House of Lords decision, which had the effect of requiring specific legislative authorization before DES could order local authorities to adopt a comprehensive secondary school program,[6] was an important precedent; its practical effect, however, was quickly vitiated by the passage of just such legislation. Uniquely with respect to busing, educational policy has been significantly shaped by the courts.

Understanding the British experience with busing puts the persisting American conflict over this issue in a usefully different light. At the least, the obvious irony— busing, a policy persistently supported by liberal Americans (and especially liberal lawyers), being undermined by Englishmen of the same stripe—warrants attention. So too does the impact of quite different approaches to the same issue, pursued by very different institutions, on the social orders of their respective countries.

Busing as the "Common Sense" Solution

Unlike the Americans, the British historically have not regarded schools as institutions designed to undo differences of social class and culture or to serve as a melting pot for the society. On the contrary: compelling different types of children to attend school together in order to produce some desired social mix has been viewed in some quarters as a profound invasion of liberty.

Writing just after the American Civil War, Robert Somers spoke for many Englishmen when he criticized required racial mixing in the schools of the American South, urged by Reconstruction leaders, as "putting the fool's cap on Republican principle."[7] A century later, J. A. Hudson, DES Deputy Secretary, declared that the department had no desire to pursue dispersal in order "to educate the community as a whole for a multi-racial, multi-cultural society," as one M.P. proposed. "Bussing is something which we would never want to undertake for its own sake. . . . I should be very surprised if we ever thought it was worth doing in order to produce a 'mix' of children which might perhaps inculcate a greater understanding of inter-racial problems."[8] Most decidedly, that was someone else's problem—if, indeed, it was a matter for public, as distinguished from private, policy.

Busing in Britain was not a carefully worked-out response to well-understood and fully anticipated events. At least in its early days, it represented a hasty reaction to a widely regretted event: the concentration of sizable numbers of nonwhite students in a handful of educational authorities. Nor did busing have deep ideological roots. Busing was not thought essential to secure racial justice, as some in the United States saw it, but rather was widely regarded as the "common sense"[9] way of coping with a perceived racial crisis, in a manner consistent with Britain's reputation for tolerence of differences. If white antagonisms made clear the need for *some* policy—and this was, in fact, the precipitating cause—the particular policy of dispersal was intended to satisfy all concerned parties, nonwhite and white. For a while, this intention was realized.

The relatively small number of nonwhites in Britain concealed the exceptional case, the community which had suddenly to reckon with a sizable minority presence. In the Midlands town of West Bromwich, for instance, the nonwhite student population grew from 492 to 737 in a fifteen-month period between 1963 and 1965; and while this was only 4.5 percent of the total student population, nonwhites were concentrated in two schools.[10] In the entire nation, fewer than ten schools were more than half nonwhite by the middle of the 1960s; but this development seemed ominous, especially to the white residents of those communities.

In no town was the issue more clearly joined than in Southall, part of the London metropolis, where substantial numbers of nonwhites, especially Sikhs from India, had settled since the late 1950s.[11] Despite the fact that nonwhites accounted for only one-fifth of the town's population, Southall itself had become visibly different. Turbaned men congregated in the streets, tandoori restaurants were beginning to replace the fish and chips establishments; a local movie theater showed exclusively Indian films. The change was most dramatically marked in one elementary school, the Beaconsfield Road School, which by 1963 had become 60 percent nonwhite, and that school was made the center of political attention. White parents organized to protest this "racial invasion"; hostilities between whites and Indians flared. The Minister of Education, Sir Edward Boyle (now Lord Boyle), dispatched to the scene, was moved to act by what he saw.

National policy was essentially crafted out of this single event. As Boyle stated in Parliament: "I must regretfully tell the House that *one school* must be regarded now as irretrievably an immigrant school. The important thing is to prevent this happening elsewhere."[12] Busing of nonwhites was generally to be the means of achieving this end. In a circular[13] issued by Anthony Crossland, Boyle's Labour successor, eighteen months after the celebrated Southall confrontation, DES spoke of the need to "spread the children":

> As the proportion of immigrant children in a school or class increases, the problems will become more difficult to solve, and the chance of assimilation more remote. . . . Up to a fifth of immigrant children in any group fit in with reasonable ease, but . . . if the proportion goes over about one third . . . serious strains emerge. It is therefore desirable that the catchment areas [attendance zone boundaries] of schools should, wherever possible, be arranged to avoid undue concentrations of immigrant children. Where this proves impracticable simply because the school serves an area which is occupied largely by immigrants, every effort should be made to disperse the immigrant children round a greater number of schools. . . .[14]

In good part, distributing minority children "thinner and wider," as Boyle had proposed, was meant to allay white fears that the academic standards and—more nebulously but no less importantly—the character of their schools would be altered by the minority presence. The only italicized paragraph of the DES circular focused on the concerns of white parents:

> It will be helpful if the parents of non-immigrant children can see that practical measures have been taken to deal with the problems in the schools, and that the progress of their own children is not being restricted by the undue preoccupation of the teaching staff with the linguistic and other difficulties of immigrant children.

If nonwhites were not bused, DES noted, "the problems within a school" could well become "so great that they cause a decline in the general standard of education provided." The converse proposition—that nonwhites might fare better, in terms of achievement, in a racially mixed school—went unvoiced. Nor was it ever seriously suggested that whites, too, be bused; there existed no sense that equity demanded a balancing of the burden of being transported to school.

Dispersal of nonwhites ensured that no school in an educational authority bore a disproportionate share of what was seen as the minority burden. The vaguely stated nature of that burden encouraged the view that racially based concerns were legitimately at issue: the DES circular referred "among other [unspecified] things, [to] the composition of the immigrant group and the number of children who are proficient in English" as the predicate for busing. The lack of any proffered educational rationale (coupled with the failure explicitly to distinguish between Asians and West Indians, whose educational needs were presumably quite different) hinted at a political rationale: busing would render the newcomers relatively invisible and hence unthreatening to whites.

This analysis tells only a part of the story. The particular beauty of dispersal—and the basis for the bipartisan and multiracial support that it initially commanded—

was not that dispersal benefited just whites, but that it also benefited nonwhites, and the society generally. For those, particularly Indians and Pakistanis, who came to school knowing little if any English, dispersal ensured immersion in an English-speaking environment, following rudimentary language instruction in special classes, and this seemed likely to speed the process of language acquisition. Regardless of the nonwhites' proficiency in English, busing made relatively painless assimilation possible, and that too was reckoned as a benefit. As the Commonwealth Immigrants Advisory Council, predecessor to the Race Relations Board, observed in 1964:

> If a school has more than a certain percentage of immigrant children among its pupils the whole character and ethos of the school is altered. Immigrant pupils will not get as good an introduction to British life as they would get in a normal school and we think that their education in the widest sense must suffer as a result.[15]

For its part, DES spoke of dispersal as enabling nonwhites to "fit in with reasonable ease. . . ." Racial invisibility, in other words, was good for nonwhites as well as whites.

Dispersal was also expected to strengthen British society as a whole, a point well understood if not convincingly articulated. Bringing nonwhite and white children together in the same schools could only improve the racial climate. Or so it was thought: this at a time when, in America, appeals to "bring us together" were eloquently expressed and deeply felt. Britain was better off remaining one community, rather than becoming a collection of separate and isolated villages; in this sense, the argument for busing echoed the argument for universalist social policy. Racial mixing in the schools would contribute to that end; racial separatism, by contrast, would likely be taken by whites as a provocation and a challenge.

Race consciousness in the short term, through the dispersal of nonwhite students, would eventually diminish attentiveness to race generally, and that was in everyone's best interest. In short, divergent arguments appealing to widely differing groups could be summoned in support of a racial dispersal policy in the schools.

The Roots of Discontent

Despite these sources of support, dispersal evoked controversy almost from its inception. Ideological vagaries, political considerations (among them the allocation of governmental authority and administrability), and consequential demographic shifts all constituted bases for objection to the practice.

Dispersal was problematic policy precisely because, after the 1965 circular, it *was* a policy pronouncement of the national government. In a nation where the allocation of responsibility between DES and local authorities is routinely cast in the vague terms of "partnership,"[16] any new DES initiative could be regarded as upsetting the prevailing balance. This is particularly the case where, as here, political homework went undone, the policy pronouncement apparently not having been preceded by the characteristic rounds of consultation with, and support-garnering from, the affected authorities. In this regard, the fact that DES only recommended dispersal, rather than insisting upon it, made little difference. For some, including the powerful National Union of Teachers, the notion that any single numerical standard could be fixed for the entire country was silliness. Immigrant education was also said to be properly the province of local officials, not of the denizens of DES.

Dispersal also presented administrative difficulties of a more mundane variety. As educators in American cities that bus students well know, managing a quota system—arranging bus contracts, identifying pick-up points, finding spare seats in the schools to which students are to be bused, mollifying irate parents—is no simple business. Determining who "needs" to be bused raises questions of a most profound sort concerning the nature of racial identification;[17] it also spawned a multitude of more routine disagreements between school officials and parents who saw busing as inappropriate for their children. Nor is busing an inexpensive enterprise: critics of dispersal argued that, over time, it would be cheaper to build new schools for minority students in their own locales than to continue sending them to distant white schools. In other words, dispersal could be seen, particularly by educators and politicians, as just too much trouble.

Educationally rooted objections were at least equally prominent. The deliberate separation of home and school created by busing was strongly at variance with the prevailing British educational wisdom that the school should forge close links with the neighborhood that it served. This point was advanced most forcefully in the Plowden Report, an influential British education policy document of the 1960s.[18] "Community schools" were to become the focus of subsequent Educational Priorities Area projects.[19] "Affirmative discrimination" intended to strengthen particular neighborhood schools, not policies that would upset neighborhood stability through student assignment to distant schools, constituted the preferred approach. Although this policy was not derived with race in mind, the Plowden Report having treated racial questions only incidentally, it had obvious ramifications for such race-specific policies as dispersal. Busing was not merely "inconvenient" for nonwhite children. Insofar as it forced them to travel to school, limited their after-school contacts, discouraged their parents from involving themselves in the life of the school and the like, it was regarded as educationally harmful.

Most disturbing, perhaps, was the perceived assault on parents' educational choice caused by dispersal. The historic significance of educational choice is reflected in the first national educational legislation, the 1870 act, which assured government support to a wide range of state and privately run schools. It is confirmed, at least symbolically, in the 1944 Education Act, which requires school officials to pay "due regard" to the wishes of parents when making school assignments.

Over time, this protection of family preference has been diminished by, among other things, the selective admission policies of the state-aided secular and religious schools; the limitation of parental choice, in the case of state-run schools, to those schools located in small attendance zones; and the substitution of comprehensive schools for the tripartite secondary education system. In a nation lacking any tradition akin to the American common school, these changes were troublesome. Restricting parental choice of school on the basis of race, as dispersal policy did, was even more troublesome. Could one seriously imagine whites surrendering their statutory right, at least to consultation, without a legal fuss? Could one even imagine whites being called upon to do so? Where attendance restrictions were based on a particular educational need, such as language instruction, the assignment policy made considerable sense, for every school could not be expected to offer the needed classes. But just what individual needs were being met by the mere fact of being a New Commonwealth Immigrant—the category promoted by DES as the basis for dispersal? Persuasive defenses of busing were not forthcoming for a people long attentive to individual liberties, distrustful of basing policy on group characteristics, and suspicious of the benefits that might be held to flow from the practice.

Unlike blacks in the United States, British minorities never demanded busing to achieve equal educational opportunity. In the main, they passively accepted the policy developed in other quarters and largely for different reasons. Nonwhites were not organized, at least in their dealing with the larger political community. They lacked both a tradition of political participation and a tradition of protest. Their collective energies were focused on economic concerns, particularly working conditions, and on maintaining social cohesiveness. Busing was, at most, of marginal concern.

Even to those who accepted the desirability of racial mixing in the schools, the very fact that dispersal was an explicit policy proved troubling. If dispersal could be carried out "naturally and easily," as the National Association of Schoolmasters urged, it was probably worth doing.[20] In that circumstance, neither questions of principle nor political embarrassments would arise. As the parliamentary Select Committee on Race Relations and Immigration noted in its 1973 report: "A considerable number of authorities" had reshaped school attendance zones and built new schools in order to "arrange that certain schools have a certain type of population";[21] to state the matter more bluntly, they had engaged in racial gerrymandering for purposes of desegregation. In Bristol, for instance, the building of schools on the outskirts of the city, away from the center of minority population, produced racial mixing without the need to resort to formal dispersal.[22] Dispersal itself was something else: the label was resisted because it called attention to a matter better left undiscussed.[23]

These sources of opposition to dispersal, taken together, undercut the DES initiative. Some education authorities—among them, Southall and West Bromwich —had begun dispersing students prior to the publication of the 1965 circular, and continued to do so. Others—including the Inner London Educational Authority (ILEA), which had the largest number of black students, and Brent, an outer London borough with the highest proportion of blacks—rejected the DES recommendation. (In the early

1970s, when approximately 30 London schools had become predominantly nonwhite, ILEA quietly explored the possibilities of boundary-manipulating, dispersal, and the like. But the issue was never formally confronted.)[24]

The discrediting of assimilation as an official government policy objective also undermined dispersal, which was supposed to facilitate assimilation. The definition of integration put forth in 1966 by Roy Jenkins, the Home Secretary, rejected assimilation in favor of "equal opportunity accompanied by cultural diversity,"[25] and in so doing, advanced a set of values at odds with the aspiration to homogenization that underlay British busing policy. A few years later, minority community representatives were treating dispersal as the whipping boy of race policy. The Afro-Caribbean Association managed to equate dispersal both with American busing and South African apartheid,[26] while the West Indian polemicist Bernard Coard likened dispersal to assignment to educationally subnormal classes, as a means of "preparing our children for society's unskilled and ill-paid jobs."[27] If none of this made for especially coherent argument, the conclusion to be drawn was unmistakeable: dispersal had lost its appeal remarkably quickly.

Not that discussions of dispersal were commonplace events. On the contrary: were it not for the Select Committee on Race Relations and Immigration harping on the matter, busing might have disappeared from public discourse. The voices that spoke up, beginning in the late 1960s, were few; what is noteworthy is that they were almost uniformly critical of the practice.

Many of the arguments for busing put forward by liberals in the United States had no counterpart in Britain. No one spoke of busing as a means of overcoming the "intentional" segregation of minorities, thus assuring them just treatment, for no one believed that minorities were intentionally segregated. In this regard, the notion that British parents could choose the school to which to send their children remained an article of policy faith even if not a present reality. A pamphlet published by the Young Fabian Society dismissed the American experience as irrelevant:

> [T]hey are trying to break down long established patterns of segregation, while here we are endeavoring to prevent such patterns forming in the first place. The immigrant concentrations [in Britain] derive from the housing problem. . . . The physical moving of schoolchildren . . . is tackling the symptoms and not the causes.[28]

Also undiscussed was the effect of desegregation on minority student achievement, an issue which the *Equal Educational Opportunity Survey*[29] (popularly known as the Coleman Report) and later, Christopher Jencks's *Inequality*[30] made central to education policy discourse in America. Achievement measures do not captivate the British to the same extent as they do Americans; the prospect of substantially raising achievement test scores for this segment of the population would thus have had no special allure.

The one extensive British study of the academic performance of minority children, carried out by ILEA, purported to test and reject the hypothesis that racial mixing improved minority achievement: "No matter how desirable for other social and educational reasons racial and ethnic mix may be, it cannot be justified in terms of the performance measures used [in this study]."[31] This conclusion cannot be fully credited in terms of the London study itself. Only a single and therefore partial measure of reading achievement, a sentence completion test, was utilized; for all that we know, other (unused) measures of achievement would have shown the effects of racial mix. Moreover, since most of London's neighborhood schools are quite homogeneous in terms of social class, such integration as existed typically involved poor nonwhites attending school with poor whites. It is at least plausible that the mixing of London's poor nonwhites and middle-class whites would have a positive impact on achievement; such an effect is suggested by American scholarship in the field.[32] But the ILEA study did not pose this policy question, and no one has subsequently proposed testing it out. The conclusion of the ILEA study—that achievement scores do not improve with desegregation—did rob dispersal's supporters of a potentially valuable argument.

A Quiet Death?

Faced with such manifest unhappiness, DES did what any organization whose leadership has failed to generate followers might be expected to do. It gradually backed off from its commitment to dispersal, leaving the policy choice firmly in the hands of local education authorities. In that way, it was thought, dispersal might die a quiet death.

By 1969, as the report of the Select Committee on Race Relations and Immigration[33] makes clear, reaction to dispersal both within DES and among members of Parliament was decidedly mixed. During the committee hearings, even as one member of parliament (M.P.) referred derisively to the dispersal formula as "very modern Boyle's Law," in apparent reference to the casual derivation of that formula, another was inquiring whether dispersal should not be made mandatory. Among the education officials who appeared at the hearings reactions were also varied. The DES Deputy Undersecretary of State, H. F. Rossetti, suggested that the department had become "rather less dogmatic" about dispersal since the publication of its circular, recognizing that "dispersal is not in all cases appropriate" and would not be the basis of "rigid policy . . . applied from the centre."[34] On the other hand,

Mr. L. J. Burrows, a senior member of H. M. Inspectorate, observed that one community's dispersal plan was regarded by "many of us [in the Inspectorate] as a model for the nation."[35] This divergence signalled the possibility that the inspectorate's advice to local education authorities might not square with DES's position.

The publication in 1971 of *The Education of Immigrants*[36] made it clear that DES had abandoned its preference for dispersal. The reasons advanced for this admittedly "significant" modification of the 1965 circular were several. The "educational need" to disperse in order to encourage the acquisition of English and acculturation was no longer seen as so compelling as in the past. Because of tightened immigration laws, fewer children now came to school unable to speak English; for those who did, other techniques, particularly the teaching of English in special classes before the onset of regular schools, were deemed preferable. Lack of familiarity with English culture might serve as a predicate for dispersing nonwhite children, DES said, but not for "isolating" them from others who shared their heritage. The increasing concentration of minorities in certain communities also rendered dispersal impractical: there were just not enough whites among whom the nonwhites could be dispersed.

Most significantly, DES was no longer as confident about the beneficial effects of dispersing minority children as it had been in 1965. DES now saw the schools as neither the primary instrument for securing "good race relations" nor "the only channel through which ideas of integration could evolve."[37] Even the desirability of integration was no longer so clear.[38] DES was only too happy to turn these matters over to the new race relations machinery that the 1968 Race Relations Act had created. Whether racial dispersal or racial concentration would "have the better influence upon future community relations" was a question "to which there may be no answer in this generation." Meanwhile, decisions concerning dispersal were left entirely to local authorities.

The politicians' opposition to dispersal found expression in the 1973 report of the Select Committee on Race Relations and Immigration. Dispersal "should now be phased out as soon as possible," undertaken only when nonwhite parents requested the chance to send their children to predominantly white schools; the burden of desegregation would be born by nonwhite individuals, rather than the educational system. In all other circumstances, "positive advances made in special provision for immigrant children" made dispersal unnecessary, the committee asserted, while "the negative effect of greatly increased numbers" of nonwhites made dispersal in any event unfeasible.[39] The evidence upon which these conclusions purportedly rested came from hearings held in Southall-Ealing, the scene of the initial *contretemps* over race and schooling a decade earlier; this fact was sufficient reminder that a policy meant to contain a racial confrontation appeared instead to have exacerbated the matter.

Other factors not noted in the formal report lay behind the policy recommendation. As one M.P. observed during the hearings:

> The reasons why busing or dispersal has not been successful or is not wanted is because invariably . . . the immigrant areas are the minority areas, and . . . the majority do not want to see immigrant children coming into their schools.[40]

Dispersal had become politically controversial. Neither DES, which in the words of then Secretary of State Margaret Thatcher "withdrew"[41] from the field, nor the members of Parliament wanted anything to do with it.

Incident in Ealing

"If the local educational authority were to be swayed by considerations [of race or color] they would . . . lay themselves open to action under the terms of the Race Relations Act 1968";[42] or so a senior DES official argued, during the 1973 Select Committee hearings. Whether this was true as a matter of statutory law was in fact never clear. As a possible scenario for the resolution of the dispersal issue, it seemed remote—almost academic—when advanced. Yet *Race Relations Board v. Ealing London Borough Council* posed precisely this question. To understand the fit between the lawsuit on the one hand and race and schooling policy on the other, one needs to appreciate both the special character of this particular community and the workings of the British antidiscrimination law enforcement apparatus.

Dispersal in the outer London borough of Ealing was initially intended to ease white concern over nonwhite concentration in certain schools; nonwhites' educational needs were scarcely noticed. Yet in operation, the enterprise turned out very differently: it afforded minority students an education markedly better than that available in their neighborhood schools. The venture that the Race Relations Board set out to dismantle through court decision became over time a model of its kind, one that many American communities might well aspire to emulate.

Dispersal in Ealing was a policy adopted by whites, and for whites. "The white children were here first": or so an Ealing councilman stated, in an unguarded moment, explaining why only nonwhite youngsters were bused. As the borough's M.P. added, dispersal itself was regarded as a way to avoid "the United States' experience with racial strife" which—without some palliative, such as dispersal—it was feared whites might emulate. This was not an altogether misdirected fear. There had been sporadic flare-ups in the schools; and so unhappy were Southall residents with the nonwhite newcomers that the health committee of the Southall City Council had, in 1963, proposed a total ban on immigration from the New Commonwealth to Britain.

Even at the outset, however, dispersal in Ealing was not just a white racist undertaking. The policy had the support of the Indian Workers' Association (IWA), the most powerful of the local immigrant groups. Indeed, representatives of the IWA had urged the Education Minister, Boyle, in drafting the DES circular, to set the ceiling on nonwhite students in any one school lower than the one-third eventually adopted. The Sikh leaders, like the whites, saw busing as a means of preserving racial harmony by defusing white hostility; they were also disinclined to challenge white opinion. But the Indian community realized that busing might well assure their children access to newer, less crowded schools and smaller classes; that it would enable their children to mingle with whites, and thus become more quickly accepted in the community; and that, in the main, the undeniable burden of busing that their children would bear might be more than compensated for in terms of educational benefits.

Of equal moment, Ealing's teachers and administrators were from the first committed to converting a politically inspired idea into one that made educational sense. The officials in charge of the dispersal effort were acknowledged national experts, and the educational program for nonwhites that they established was among the best in the country, a splendid example of positive discrimination. In 1972–73, Ealing obtained 15.80 pounds in Local Government Act funds for each child labelled "New Commonwealth Immigrant," one of the highest per pupil figures in the country.[43] This money was used imaginatively. Many of the entering nonwhite students were assigned to an assessment center, where their educational needs—particularly with respect to language—were explored in detail; this assessment was used in making subsequent class assignments. In the schools to which the students were bused, special language classes offered basic English instruction for a period ranging from six months to two years; when subsequently placed in the regular classroom, the students had considerable familiarity with English. The regular classes themselves were treated as settings for continued language instruction, for it was felt that constant exposure to English as naturally spoken could only improve comprehension. Both the elaborate assessment, unique in Britain, and this link between special program and regular classroom experience made possible by dispersal drew praise from professional observers.

Other efforts undertaken by Ealing were consistent with the educators' commitment to nonwhite students. For those who had come to Ealing late in their educational careers and who began work not knowing English, a full-time training center called the Pathways Programme was established. Subsequently, in cooperation with DES, the authority moved directly into the factories, its Industrial Language Centre offering basic instruction to workers on a released-time basis. Although such undertakings may be regarded as merely training compliant, low-status workers (even though the curricula of both centers call attention to the workers' rights, in a manner sometimes galling to employers), the efforts are better seen as responses to the specific and expressed desires of a community more interested in jobs than ideology.

Ealing was also anxious to help nonwhite students at the top of the educational ladder. In 1970, 30 nonwhites whose grades would not have entitled them to admission to the Southall Grammar School were nonetheless enrolled on the basis of their intellectual promise. That these students did well, and that the experiment was abandoned only because Ealing adopted a comprehensive secondary school system, matters less than what the undertaking itself reveals; namely, that Ealing was demonstrably willing to take what in Britain are extraordinary measures on behalf of nonwhites.

These ventures became the source of considerable pride to a Labour-dominated borough council. The initial racist motivation for busing nonwhite students receded into history. Dispersal evolved into liberal policy, and a readily understandable revisionism concerning its origins encouraged the viewpoint that busing had always been undertaken on behalf of nonwhites. Council members saw their actions as benign, not benighted. When queried in 1975, the education authority asserted that, in busing minority students, it was complying with DES's recommendation that all immigrant children be made "fully familiar" with the English language and way of life. The interests of whites had completely dropped out of the picture.

Maurice Kogan, Professor of Government and Social Administration at Brunel University and a former senior DES official, reviewed Ealing's dispersal efforts on behalf of the Race Relations Board in 1975. His report praised the program highly.[44] The schools to which nonwhites were bused were characterized by their "graciousness of environment," a sharp contrast with the overcrowded Dickens-era buildings in Southall. And the education that nonwhites received was superb. "The schools which I saw were fully up to the general range of the schools . . . presented as examples of the best of British primary education, when I worked on the Plowden Committee."

Most vitally, in terms of improving race relations the undertaking seemed a signal success. The bused children had merged into their new environment so naturally and completely that, as Kogan reported, teachers repeatedly had to be reminded that these were, in fact, nonwhite immigrants. Kogan's major conclusion reads as a paean to this "exemplary" enterprise:

> Here is one group of schools in which teachers are positively arresting disadvantage and creating a cohesive and integrated society through what they are doing in the schools. . . . No case of discriminatory practice, other than positive and benign dis-

> crimination, can rest against the educational process being employed in these schools.

What more could any education authority be expected to achieve?

Despite these achievements, large segments of Ealing's liberal and minority community came to regard dispersal as discriminatory. Although the Indian Social Club president (former secretary of the IWA) argued that opposing dispersal was "equivalent to placing a tool in the hands of the racialist," by the early 1970s this was decidedly the deviant viewpoint. The local Community Relations Council, perhaps the most political of such institutions in the country, called in 1968 for the gradual phasing out of dispersal; subsequently the council urged its prompt termination.[45] When the Select Committee on Race Relations and Immigration went to Ealing in 1973 to discuss dispersal, organized reaction was almost wholly negative. The IWA had sometime earlier changed its position, and now opposed dispersal; so too did the Southall Communist Party (led by a former IWA president; factionalism in the IWA was commonplace). One year later, running on a platform that prominently featured opposition to dispersal, the Communist party ticket did uncharacteristically well in Southall's elections, nearly winning two seats. Opposition to dispersal was not confined to community leaders.[46] The Ealing Community Relations Council reported that, in an informal poll, both Indians and Pakistanis favored racially mixed schools but opposed compulsory busing; West Indians in the community perceived busing as an "insult."

Busing, its opponents said, denied nonwhite parents choices available to whites. The policy had also perpetuated "the long-standing neglect of education throughout the [Southall] borough";[47] Ealing got the new schools, while Southall children rode buses, and hence were treated unequally. In the end, all of the educational justifications for dispersal as practiced in Ealing could not overcome this fatal flaw: even if bused students received "better" schooling, race and not educational need was the basis upon which busing determinations were made. Professor Kogan's assessment made the same point, in expressing concern about the "indeterminate number" of students bused despite their proficiency in English: Were they not the victims of unlawful discrimination?

Ealing school officials and council members were also having second thoughts about dispersal. While the Ealing Director of Education stated to the Select Committee that dispersal aided language acquisition and permitted nonwhites to become familiar with British "culture and lore," he added that the borough was planning to build new schools in Southall, thus permitting a drastic reduction in the number of dispersed pupils. In December 1974, the Ealing Borough Council voted to abandon dispersal "as soon as practicable."

Changing demography made this political reappraisal almost inevitable. In 1963, at the onset of dispersal, nonwhites constituted substantially less than 10 percent of the student population (by 1966, the first year for which figures are available, they numbered 4,300, 11.5 percent of the student body). Ten years later, there were 11,900 "immigrants" (as defined by DES), over one-quarter of the student population, while nonwhites (as estimated by Ealing) represented over 30 percent.[48] As nonwhite enrollment grew, the education authority first relaxed the percentage limitation on immigrant enrollment fixed in the 1965 DES circular, but this was merely a temporary expedient. There are "too few English children without bussing them in to keep the proportion [of whites] up," the Ealing superintendent reported to the Select Committee. "Bussing [whites] in" was not politically possible, and requests that neighboring boroughs admit some of Ealings's nonwhites to their schools had earlier been rejected.

In the face of these altered circumstances, the superintendent indicated that continuing support for dispersal was largely premised on practical considerations. There just were not enough Southall neighborhood schools to house all the minority students. The persistent drumfire of community opposition to dispersal had had a cumulative effect: building new schools in Southall now seemed a politically easier course of action than trying somehow to press on with busing.

Dispersal would be phased out in Ealing; about that, there was a consensus. The salient question was when this would happen. By the time the Select Committee and, subsequently, Professor Kogan came to Ealing, what had once been a vigorous ideological dispute over the merits of busing had been transformed into rather more pragmatic bargaining over the timing of an agreed-upon policy change and the number of new schools required to accomplish it.[49] Having convinced DES to let it build new schools in Southall despite the availability of empty classroom space elsewhere in the authority, Ealing was proposing to complete three buildings by 1981. The minority community groups wanted more schools constructed more rapidly in order to eliminate all busing. This is not, one might conclude, the ideal setting for a test case challenging the legality of a racially based busing policy— especially since there existed other British communities whose enthusiasm for dispersal had not dissipated.

Legalizing the Dispersal Issue

Resolution of the dispersal dispute through the courts was, from the outset, highly improbable. The argument that dispersal discriminates against racial minority students within the terms of the 1968 Race Relations Act (or its 1976 successor) is devilishly difficult. Moreover, the enforcing agency, the Race Relations Board (RRB), never showed much inclination to tackle difficult cases, particularly where these involved suits against governmental units. Both obstacles to bringing litigation were surmounted, in what for Britain represents a rare triumph for the legalistic and confrontationist, as distinguished from the political and ameliorative, approach to allegations of discrimination.

The 1968 Race Relations Act defined discrimination in terms of "less favourable" treatment on grounds of race or ethnic origin. Refusal to provide services "of like quality, in like manner" was one type of prohibited discriminatory treatment. Could dispersal be so described? Dispersed students were not treated "in like manner," as compared with those not dispersed; and, since only nonwhite immigrants were dispersed, the practice could be viewed as based on race. Yet might not any busing scheme be defended as premised on educational need—whether for language acquisition or, more nebulously, acculturation to British "culture and lore"—rather than on race. If so, the chances for a successful defense appeared excellent. In *Cumings v. Birkenhead*,[50] Lord Denning, writing for the Court of Appeals, declared that a student assignment policy based on "valid educational reasons" would be upheld against a claim of discrimination; only if the enterprise was "so unreasonable that no reasonable authority could entertain it" would a court intervene. Busing does not readily fit within this narrow definition of unreasonableness.

Moreover, even if one were candidly to admit that race was the reason for dispersal, might it not be said that, in being sent to predominantly white schools, nonwhites were if anything being treated *more* favorably because of their race? Under the 1968 Race Relations Act, segregation always constituted "unfavourable" treatment; what about the converse proposition, that desegregation was not the sort of race-consciousness against which the act was directed?

The major commentary on the legislation, *Race and Law in Great Britain,* temporized on this question.[51] Dispersal "might" contravene the law, the authors (the Race Relations Board's barrister and solicitor) concluded. If students were bused on the basis of race from a "good local comprehensive school . . . to an inferior secondary school," this would add an element of disadvantage that could be described as discriminatory. The point was valid, but the facts in Ealing were readily distinguishable. There, the question might be phrased: Was busing that added an element of advantage also discriminatory?

In this respect, the 1976 Race Relations Act makes the legal task of equating dispersal with discrimination all the more difficult. That law, while retaining the definition of discrimination as less favorable treatment, treats as nondiscriminatory "any act done in affording persons of a particular racial group access to facilities or services to meet the *special needs* of persons of that group in regard to their education. . . ." The provision does not specify that the affected group, as distinguished from the government, determine whether needs are special. Busing can readily be defended in just these terms, as responding to the "special needs" of minority school children.

If this doctrinal quagmire was not enough to dampen enthusiasm for a lawsuit, other factors added to the improbability of RRB involvement. Were the board to intercede, it would be challenging the legality of a local authority's action, something it almost never did; suits against dance halls accused of denying admission to nonwhites were more its sort of case than litigation against the government. Moreover, no Ealing resident had complained about dispersal to the board. For the board to act, it would have to initiate the proceedings on its own, a statutorily permissible but seldom adopted course of action.[52]

At every stage, the RRB pursued Ealing with uncharacteristic zeal.[53] It decided to investigate dispersal after an Indian-born member of the board recounted objections to dispersal in Ealing voiced on a Sunday morning Hindustani-language television program. The board did not use its own staff to conduct the investigation, but instead appointed an outside professional, Maurice Kogan, to do the job. It chose to publicize Professor Kogan's report, an unprecedented action which dampened the prospects for quiet settlement and increased the likelihood of an eventual confrontation. There were no extensive negotiations with Ealing: only a few months elapsed between the formal RRB finding that, on the basis of the Kogan report, busing in Ealing was discriminatory insofar as it was predicated on race and the filing of the lawsuit in 1976. Neither during that time nor in framing the case did the board urge Ealing to adopt a busing plan involving both whites and nonwhites, despite an earlier opinion from its own solicitor that "busing of both blacks and whites would not be discriminatory."

Most astonishingly, the case was filed despite the board's inability to identify a single child who was injured by the practice of dispersal and willing to join the suit. Of the twelve bused children interviewed in Ealing by the board's staff as possible plaintiffs, nine spoke no English prior to entering school, and thus could well have been bused on educational grounds, not because they were nonwhite. In the other three instances, the board concluded that it would be impossible to prove that, prior to schooling, the child was proficient in English. This did not daunt the board's counsel. While there must be a victim for discrimination to occur, the RRB's barrister argued, it was not essential that the victim be identified. Racial discrimination was the natural and probable consequence of Ealing's practice, he added, even if no actual injury could be shown.[54]

The Ealing case constitutes a most extraordinary adventure for the Race Relations Board, an institution more used to polite persuasion than legal arm twisting. This point may be better appreciated by contrasting the Ealing events with the board's gingerly treatment of two other potential busing disputes involving the two north country cities of Blackburn and Bradford.

Like Ealing, Blackburn and Bradford dispersed only nonwhite students. Just 120 students were dispersed in Blackburn, but at least 1,400 (out of a total nonwhite student population of 10,000) were dispersed in Bradford. Complaints from both cities were filed with the board; to the RRB's embarrassment, the complaining party in each instance was not a nonwhite but a member of the fascist National Front. The complaint in Blackburn claimed that, by giving nonwhites but not whites buses to ride, dispersal amounted to reverse discrimination. The Bradford complaint was more sophisticated, asserting that busing cost nonwhite children valuable time, denied them a neighborhood school, and angered minority parents. That these assertions could just as well have been made by the IWA as by the National Front added an ironic touch.

The board appointed a linguistics expert, Professor Eric Hawkins of York University, to review the Blackburn situation. Hawkins, unlike Kogan, interpreted his mandate narrowly. Without discussing at any length the quality of education offered to nonwhites in Blackburn, his 1973 report concluded that dispersal was premised on language deficiencies, not race. This was new policy in Bradford, where a short time earlier teachers had reported that one-quarter of the bused students did not have language problems. The Director of Education in Blackburn admitted as much: "In our enthusiasm to do the right thing by immigrant pupils and, in addition, to 'protect' the education of English pupils in these schools, we may have committed a breach of the Race Relations Act" by busing students for racial reasons.

The refusal of the religious schools to admit a proportionate share of nonwhite students made some busing inevitable, Professor Hawkins observed; there just was not enough space in the neighborhood schools for all residents. Of greatest significance, Blackburn had had a change of heart about dispersal early in the 1970s, when a Labour majority came to power. The new city council was only too happy to discuss with Professor Hawkins ways of eliminating anything that might be termed discriminatory. At that juncture, the case disappeared from board purview.

The situation in Bradford was very different.[55] There, the education authority created a working party to review its dispersal program. Its 1976 report unanimously recommended the continuation of busing. Dispersal, the report noted, has been:

> consistently regarded . . . as an essential and integral part of the system of comprehensive measures being taken to ensure that as far as possible children of immigrant parents overcome their initial disadvantage and receive educational opportunities equal to those of children of indigenous parents.[56]

The aim of dispersal, the report acknowledged, was to "submerge" the differences "by the similarities. It is considered more likely that harmonious race relations in our future multi-racial city will be encouraged in this way than if 'blacks' and 'whites' were educated separately and seldom meet." Dispersal encouraged "cross-fertilization"; the alternative of permitting racially identifiable schools to operate would only lead to a "lowering of standards, a retreat into closed communities."

Here was a community whose commitment to dispersal was, if anything, stronger than Ealing's, and whose views were certainly not the handmaiden of national fashion. Yet the RRB managed to avoid taking any position on the case. It dispatched Professor Hawkins, who had reviewed the Blackburn situation, to Bradford. As in Blackburn, Hawkins conceived his task narrowly, focusing not on the desirability of dispersal but on whether dispersal as practiced in Bradford could be justified in terms of language instruction needs rather than race. The only subject of Professor Hawkins's inquiry was the screening process, which he concluded was generally satisfactory. In response to Hawkins's critique, Bradford modestly altered its practice. Meanwhile, the Commission for Racial Equality (whose predecessor, the RRB, had commissioned the investigation) had so lost interest that it did not, as anticipated, request a follow-up report from Professor Hawkins. The commission, Hawkins noted, was apparently "letting the matter lie."[57]

Ealing embodied a special set of circumstances, a point recognized as early as May 1972, when a General Committee Report of the Race Relations Board noted that to take on the case would stir up "a live political issue, resulting in a hardening of attitudes toward this question." That Ealing represented the exceptional case was clear from an October 1976 staff report to the board concerning Bradford. "I do not suppose that the Board, after the Ealing experience, will want to get enmeshed too deeply in other local [dispersal] issues."

Throughout the Ealing affray, the legalistic staff and counsel of the board pushed for RRB action against what seemed not only discriminatory conduct, but consequential discriminatory conduct. That view seldom prevailed in an agency reluctant to stir up a "live political issue." That it did prevail on this occasion had much to do with Ealing itself. The authority had consistently sparred with the board; more galling, Ealing had actually bested the RRB in one of the handful of discrimination cases to reach the House of Lords.[58]

Ealing's obduracy—or, as some might have it, keen lawyering—was evident in the early stages of the busing case. Reconciliation proposed by Sir Geoffrey Wilson, Chairman of the RRB, was undermined, apparently by the Ealing solicitor. The litigation phase of the dispute at times resembled *Jarndyce v. Jarndyce*, Dickens's nightmare vision of a never-ending lawsuit. Requests for "further and better particulars" were followed by demands for "particulars on particulars," a strategy calculated to keep the lawyers busy and slow down the pace of the lawsuit.

Only because of a breakdown in the political and bureaucratic system within which British race and education policy is customarily made did dispersal even reach the courts. The British judiciary never had the opportunity to address the merits of the case. Both on trial and on appeal, Ealing did not enter a substantive defense of its position. Instead, the authority relied on procedural arguments. The absence of a named complainant, someone actually hurt by dispersal, was said to be inconsistent with the requisites of a legal "case"; the "oppressive" nature of the demand for information (the defense conjuring up an obligation to review millions of documents) was asserted as another ground for dismissal.[59] In 1977, these questions were resolved against Ealing by the Court of Appeals,[60] thus clearing the way for inquiry into whether busing as practiced in Ealing is racially discriminatory.

The courts will not, however, determine the permissibility of busing. In a 1978 settlement, proposed by a newly elected Conservative council, Ealing agreed to disperse students entering school only on grounds of demonstrated educational need, not race. The actual impact of this policy change in Ealing will be modest and short-lived because the authority is constructing new schools in the Southall neighborhoods of Ealing where nonwhites live.[61] The underlying legal question—is busing statutorily permissible?—remains unresolved.

Busing in Britain: The Demise of a Racially Explicit Policy

Busing was supposed to be all things to all men. It held out to the white majority the promise of preserving the character of British schools; to nonwhites, it offered the potential of speedy and painless integration; to the society as a whole, it bespoke the universalist value of a coherent British community. Within a few short years of its adoption, none of those rationales seemed politically persuasive. The supporters of busing had vanished into the woodwork. Its opponents branded the practice a racial insult. The racial explicitness of dispersal, essential to its operation, came to constitute the cause of its demise.

In a sense, even had the court definitively resolved the busing issue, the Ealing suit would have had little policy relevance. Dispersal had been repudiated in all but a handful of educational authorities well before the case was brought. Indeed, it may be that the suit could have been brought only because substantive issues had already been resolved as a consensual political matter. The consequence of this policy *volte face* concerning dispersal should not go unrecognized. In an increasing if currently uncounted number of schools, nonwhites predominate. The nearly all-minority school, although not yet a widespread reality, may soon become so.

From the beginning, the hope was that this eventuality would be avoided, not through reassigning students but through fostering racially mixed housing. The fact that, in Britain, public housing accounts for nearly one-third of the housing stock made this aspiration at least theoretically possible. As the 1965 *White Paper on Immigration from the Commonwealth* declared:

> It will become commonplace for Commonwealth immigrants to be rehoused by local authorities in pursuance of their normal statutory responsibilities. This in itself will tend to break up excessive and undesirable concentrations.[62]

The Young Fabians had said much the same thing in urging that attention be focused on the cause of racial separation—housing—rather than on the symptom—racial concentration in the schools.[63]

That was not to be. Dispersal in housing did not come naturally. Deliberate dispersal has disappeared as a policy goal, for reasons similar to those underlying the demise of dispersal in education: such efforts intruded on individual liberty, resting that intrusion on the socially unacceptable basis of race.

A 1969 government report reveals the then prevailing policy schizophrenia.[64] Housing dispersal should not be made compulsory, the report declared, because "this would involve treating people as things. . . . Dispersal is a laudable aim of policy but this policy needs pursuing with full respect for the wishes of the people concerned." Yet if dispersal were not undertaken, the report recognized, racial concentrations could only yield an "intensification of disadvantage." That price has apparently been judged worth paying by liberal Britons. A May 1977 report of the Community Relations Commission on housing opposed efforts to disperse as inconsistent with honoring family choice; about the adverse consequences of racial concentration, the report was silent.[65]

Dispersal continues both in education and housing; it is just not so labelled. In local educational authorities and local housing agencies, efforts persist "to secure . . . the effective dispersal of black immigrant clientele without, however, having formally to acknowledge that any deliberate dispersal of either immigrant school children or immigrant council tenants had ever in principle been decided upon."[66] It is the explicitness of dispersal, not dispersal itself, that is widely regarded as unacceptable.[67]

This is a familiar story in the annals of British race policy generally, and race and schooling policy particularly. Racial issues are confronted only inexplicitly, as by subsuming them in the problems of immigrants, deprived urban villagers, or what have you; or, as with dispersal, undertaking quietly what must be denied if ever brought to public attention. Government does nothing, or at least does nothing overtly, with regard to race. No one knows how much dispersal of British nonwhite students actually goes on, and that is just the way authorities prefer it.

There is much to be said in favor of this point of view, with respect to dispersal and to race and schooling policy more broadly. But in cities such as London, where dispersal has not been quietly achieved (and therefore has not been achieved at all), the inevitable result is the emergence in minority-dominated neighborhoods of what can only be termed ghetto schools, which provide an education equally as unsatisfactory as many American schools functioning in similar circumstances.[68] In Washington, D.C. or Detroit, one does not inquire whether ghetto schools are good or bad, as such. Given the proportion of blacks in the school district, such schools are inevitable. This is not the case in London. Because nonwhites remain less than 30 percent of the school-age population, and because nonwhites and whites live in comparatively close proximity, nonwhites could as a logistical matter be assigned to desegregated schools relatively easily.

One assessment of race relations in British communities found most to praise in Bradford, the only town that has adhered to a policy of explicitly dispersing nonwhite students. "The city continues to be the standing refutation of the argument that multiracial communities are inevitably beset by racial troubles."[69] Yet in this study, Bradford did not emerge as an ideal community. Nonwhites and whites coexisted, it was said, with "highly unequal interracial accommodation." Insofar as dispersal in Bradford stressed the adjustments that nonwhites have to make, it doubtless contributed something to that circumstance as well.

This ambiguous report on Bradford only further muddles the policy problem. The British race policy norm of inexplicitness can be perceived as embodying a lack of caring. On the other hand, racially explicit policies such as dispersal may be seen as merely paternalistic caring or caring for unequals. Much the same point may be made about the American educational policy of leaving black enclaves to their "natural" fate or, pursuant to court order, breaking up those enclaves by busing students to distant schools with scant regard for notions of community or choice.[70] The pitfalls of present practice are more readily identified than new policy approaches. Is there a way out of this policy *cul de sac*?

four

Toward an Appraisal of Racial Explicitness

Most policy decisions, Edmund Burke observed, involve not the happy discovery of a social panacea but rather the less happy task of choosing between the disagreeable and the intolerable; that is a useful caution to bear in mind, in reviewing and assessing the workings of inexplicitness as public policy in Britain.

This chapter approaches the necessarily speculative task of assessment from several vantages. It first reviews the experience in the educational policy arena, then broadens the scope of inquiry to encompass British social policy generally. In both contexts, the policy question to be addressed is: How well has inexplicitness worked? A full assessment of that question demands a comparison between alternatives, contending policies, and for that reason the concluding section of the chapter juxtaposes the relevant American and British racial policy histories.

Inexplicitness and Schooling

In the domain of education, the consequences of pursuing a policy of inexplicitness have varied with the substantive issue. In certain instances, inexplicitness implies doing nothing. Thus, DES has not kept track of the number of nonwhite students, opposes suggestions that a categorical aid program be created to address their particular needs, and expresses concern over curricular efforts that stress the salience of race or ethnicity; and the Race Relations Board and its successor, the Commission for Racial Equality, seek to abolish dispersal of nonwhites on the grounds that the practice draws distinctions along impermissible racial lines.

In other instances, inexplicitness means aiding nonwhites with seeming inadvertence, doing good by stealth. The English language instructional programs best exemplify this second meaning: nonwhites are the primary beneficiaries of language instruction, even though need, not race, is the predicate for this assistance. The various government programs aiding local authorities with special needs benefit nonwhites, albeit modestly, for nonwhites constitute part of the larger category of disadvantaged or socially needy children; this consequence is understood, if nowhere spelled out in the legislation. Student dispersal as an instrument of educational policy may be officially dead, but some education authorities take the racial composition of neighborhoods into account, in order to encourage racial mixing, when drawing school attendance boundaries; that practice too reveals inexplicitness at work.

The very fact that race policy is inexplicit makes conventional evaluation difficult. By some measures, nonwhites appear to have fared relatively better in British schools in recent years. Substantially fewer are described as having language difficulties,[1] although this change could be predicted from the dramatically declining proportion of nonwhite children who are themselves immigrants. More interestingly, one study found that nonwhite children who had been enrolled in British schools from the beginning of their educational careers performed considerably better than those who came from overseas; even this group, however, performed well below the norm.[2]

With respect to other policy-relevant questions—the relative proportion of nonwhites who take A-level (advanced secondary school) examinations or pursue post-secondary schooling, for instance—one has only the hunch that nonwhites are less successful than whites, and that, among the nonwhites, West Indians fare worst. Similarly, concerning the concentration of nonwhites in particular schools—a relevant fact, if one believes that educational or social benefits derive from racial mixing—one can only surmise from the general growth in the number of nonwhites in Britain, and from anecdotal reports, that there are more nonwhite students and that they increasingly congregate in a relatively small number of schools. No published data exist to confirm or disprove these speculations concerning minority achievement or racial isolation, a circumstance attributable to the pursuit of inexplicitness.

Given this paucity of data, what one makes of British race and educational policy partly depends on what one anticipates to be achievable through schooling reform. Traditionally, the British have not regarded education as a primary instrument of social and economic mobility. There have, however, been those, steeped in the tradition of Fabian Socialism, who have adhered to a more optimistic view of the powers of schooling;[3] and this position has become increasingly popular in the wake of the postwar British social revolution. Some British liberals anticipated that comprehensive schools, in conjunction with other social reforms, would erode long-standing social class differences. With respect to race, the hope was much the same: the "second generation" of nonwhites, those educated in Britain, "would grow up to be 'coloured English children,'"[4] indistinguishable from their white counterparts. Such hopes were understandable and by no means novel. They mirrored the views of American common school advocates expressed more than a century earlier, as well as the aspirations of those who latterly sought to undo racial segregation in American public schools.

In practice, these expectations have been largely frustrated. If social class lines in Britain have become more permeable since World War II, class differentiation nonetheless remains a prominent feature of British life; nor have the nonwhite youths disappeared into the larger population after leaving school. Moreover, it is unclear how much impact schooling reform has had on either racial or social class inequities. It turns out, for example, that although more individuals from all social strata have graduated from British universities in the years since the 1944 Education Act—no surprise, given the larger number of university places—the gap in the proportion of upper and lower class British graduates has actually increased, and possession of the university degree has assumed greater importance in acquiring one's first job.[5] The greater availability of advanced education has not furthered equalization, but only confirmed the old policy adage, "the more the more."

One response to such disappointing findings is to blame the schools for failing in their task, and a considerable amount of blaming has taken place. Comprehensive schools have been faulted for recreating academic, and hence social, stratification. DES policy with respect to race has been dismissed in a *Times Educational Supplement* article as "daft."

These critics may well be imposing on the British educational system (if one can describe that amorphous enterprise in such precise terms) a burden that it cannot bear.[6] Schooling has historically confirmed the prevailing social order, not remade it. Where conflict concerning values is detectable, as with respect to questions of race and class in Britain, that conflict will almost inevitably find its counterpart in the ambiguities of the educational experience. Moreover, the central task of an educational system, at least in a democratic state, has less to do with shaping social relations or race relations than with furthering literacy and numeracy and developing clear habits of mind. How schools could act directly to improve racial relations is most uncertain; to propose that they do so, without linking that effort to the intellectual purpose of the enterprise, makes little apparent sense.

In assessing the effects of inexplicitness, the first wisdom is the counsel of modesty; one recalls the Danish sailor in Melville's *Billy Budd*, who after many years had learned "that bitter prudence which never interferes with aught, and never gives advice."[7] Whatever policy DES might adopt, no one should expect that the British educational system will overcome all of the divisions between nonwhites and whites or the effects of those divisions on their children: at least, it will not do so without substantial support from other quarters, public and private, and not in the blink of an eye that, in terms of history, marks the period of nonwhite presence in Britain. As the National Association of Schoolmasters observed in a 1973 memorandum submitted to the parliamentary Select Committee on Race Relations and Immigration: "We do not think that it is reasonable for the schools to be expected to make more than a peripheral contribution towards the solution of the general social problem."[8] But modesty need not betoken policy abdication. Doing good does not imply doing nothing. Would a more racially explicit policy have reaped greater gains?

Inexplicitness as Social Policy

Inexplicitness and "Benign Neglect." One way of comprehending Britain's race policy experience is by contrasting it with a telling episode in American civil rights history. At the very beginning of the 1970s, when in America the subject of race seemed capable of generating not enlightenment but only the fiercest of antagonisms, Daniel P. Moynihan, then counselor to President Nixon, urged the inauguration of a period of "benign neglect."

> The subject has been too much talked about. The forum has been too much taken over to hysterics, paranoids and boddlers on all sides. We may need a period in which Negro progress continues and racial rhetoric fades.[9]

Blacks had been in the policy forefront for much of the preceding decade, but they perceived themselves as badly treated by the Nixon administration. To the American black leadership, already deeply displeased with Nixon's performance, Moynihan's proposal provoked outrage. Neglect, whether benign or otherwise, was viewed as the very worst approach to racial issues. Twenty-one leaders of the black movement, representing an impressively broad spectrum of organizations, condemned the statement as a "calculated, aggressive and systematic effort . . . to wipe out all the civil rights gains made in the 1950s and 1960s."[10]

Taken in context, and rather more dispassionately, the Moynihan suggestion meant no such thing. There was not a hint in the memorandum that programs that benefited blacks be abandoned, only that the rhetoric of race be moderated. In attempting clarification, Moynihan spoke of "solidify[ing] the gains of the sixties. . . ."[11] (Moynihan might have, but did not, note that when Edmund Burke spoke in praise of "a wise and salutory neglect," he did so in the context of urging that Britain grant the American colonies' wish for independence.)[12] But clarification proved futile. Phrases assume lives of their own, and this came to symbolize white political callousness. Once exposed to bright light, benign neglect could not survive: this was a policy suggestion whose very existence depended upon circumspection.

The circumstances in Britain have been rather more propitious for such an approach. The influence of race on electoral politics has been sporadic and, at least until now, never vital. "Softness" on race may well have cost one prospective Labour Party cabinet member his seat in the 1964 elections—his successful conservative opponent campaigned on the slogan, "If you want a nigger neighbor, vote Labour"—but this event evoked so much notice because of its rarity. The fascist National Front, which calls for the repatriation of nonwhites, has attracted more attention than votes.[13] Enoch Powell, a genuinely popular figure, upset the Conservative Party leadership with his envisioned "rivers of blood" and appalled that leadership with his call for repatriation of nonwhites but has had no sustained political impact. While Conservative Party leader Margaret Thatcher's recent vow of a "clear end to immigration" in order to keep "the British character" from being "swamped by people with a different culture" is premised on the assumption that race has more than marginal political significance in Britain, the ultimate impact of Thatcher's foray remains uncertain.[14] Nor has race been so central an element of private policy as in the United States. Although the level of racial tension has from time to time been high—the annual carnival at Notting Hill has become an occasion for racial violence—Britain has witnessed nothing resembling the riots in Detroit or Watts (or New York City, when the lights went out). Minority rhetoric has, by American standards, been muted.

The nonwhite population remains small (about 3 percent), new, and concentrated in a relative handful of places.[15] It counts for less than its American counterpart. Moderate nonwhite leaders are drawn into the British establishment—there are, most noticeably, two nonwhite peers in the House of Lords—and nonwhite radicals are typically treated just as Moynihan urged, by being ignored. As one unhappy activist declared: "Revolution does not come out of the sleeve of a dashiki."[16] Racial inexplicitness, as British policy makers have quietly practiced it, has a way of making words like "revolution" sound the merest nonsense. Without ever saying so (rather, because they never said so), the British have managed to convert Moynihan's prescription for "benign neglect" into policy fact.

Appraising the Record. How has inexplicitness fared, not with respect to education but more generally as social policy? There can, of course, be no straightforward answer to that question. Even if we could somehow splice history as if it were a film, introducing a policy of determined racial explicitness in lieu of the inexplicit path actually taken and rerunning the film, disagreements would inevitably arise concerning the nature of success. All that we can in fact do is to assess various measures of performance under one policy regime.

Those assessments tell a story of considerable progress, a fact that should surprise only those to whom Cassandra-like utterances come naturally.[17] The story is not unmixed. There are indications of regress as well as of progress (as in the particularly hostile attitudes toward nonwhites now held by those between the ages of 16 and 29).[18] No one could seriously claim that racial minorities enjoy equal conditions or possess equal status with British whites. There does remain a substantial problem. But there is less of a problem, in certain key respects, than was true a decade ago.

Attitude surveys suggest how racial matters are perceived by the populace generally. Since 1959, the British have been asked whether "feeling between white and coloured people is getting better or worse."[19] In 1975, 32 percent detected improvement, 20 percent slippage; 37 percent saw no change (the balance expressed no opinion). This set of replies does not paint the rosiest of pictures. Yet it is substantially more optimistic than any of the earlier survey responses. In 1959, for instance, only one in six Britons reported improvement, while 44 percent saw worsening; in 1965, the comparable figures were 18 and 39 percent; in 1973, 24 and 33 percent. The survey records consistently greater optimism over time, with the exception of a poll conducted immediately after Enoch Powell's famous 1968 "rivers of blood" speech. Nonwhites, queried specially in 1975, were even more positive about racial attitudes than the general populace: 44 percent reported that relationships were improving, only 13 percent suggested that they were getting worse.

White Britons also distinguish between "coloured immigrants" and "coloured people," a distinction that suggests something about the shape of race relations over time. Their ambivalence as hosts has persisted, but they report substantially greater "sympathy" for nonwhites who are also British by birth.[20] In a 1976 survey, their sympathy for "coloured immigrants" was 48.8, almost halfway between completely sympathetic and completely unsympathetic—rather more sympathetic than toward the Labour Party, a bit less than toward the Conservatives. Toward "coloured people born in Britain," the comparable sympathy figure was 70.1—a number higher than for both the trade unions and the political parties, but lower than for the police.

With respect to basic needs for housing and jobs, surveys record a positive shift in nonwhite perceptions of British even-handedness. When queried in 1974, fewer nonwhites believed that discrimination in housing or employment was widespread as compared with 1966–67 findings.[21] Among West Indians, 73 percent did state that employers discriminate on the basis of race. This is an alarmingly high proportion, but lower than the 87 percent who responded affirmatively in the earlier survey. Among Pakistanis and Indians, the decline was similar; from 58 to 40 percent, in the case of Pakistanis, and from 73 to 50 percent among the Indians. More interestingly, the sharpest decline comes among those who claim personal experience with discrimination: in the 1966–67 survey, 45 percent of West Indians asserted that they had suffered employment discrimination; in 1974, that number had dropped to only 16 percent. Similar changes are reported for the other two groups. If discrimination persists, it is to a considerable extent something that others are being victimized by.

Views concerning housing discrimination have evolved in a similar fashion.[22] In 1966–67, 88 percent of West Indians stated that landlords discriminate on the basis of race; 39 percent of those responses were drawn from personal experience. Seven years later, 74 percent of the West Indians adhered to this point of view, but by then only one in five had personally been victimized. For Pakistanis and Indians, the change is comparable. Particularly acute is the drop among those who have themselves suffered discrimination: just 6 percent of Pakistanis and 8 percent of Indians make this claim.

Actual tests of employment and housing practices conducted by Political and Economic Planning (PEP) support the proposition that the incidence of discrimination has in fact declined. When in 1974 nonwhite testers applied for manual jobs, 37 percent were turned away on the basis of race; with respect to skilled jobs, the comparable figure was 20 percent. Of those applying by letter for white-collar jobs, 30 percent of the nonwhite testers were turned away, where whites were invited for an interview.[23] No precise comparison can be made with the 1967 study, which focused only on firms against which complaint of discrimination had already been lodged: there, testing corroborated the complaints, revealing that discrimination against the nonwhite occurred 90 percent of the time.[24]

With respect to housing, comparisons over time can be made, and these are encouraging.[25] In telephone testing concerning rental housing, conducted by West Indian testers in 1967 and West Indians and Asians in 1974, reports of discrimination declined from 62 to 27 percent. Personal visits concerning home purchase produced discriminatory behavior in 64 percent of all cases in 1967, as compared with 29 percent in 1974 (and that latter figure includes 17 percent of all interviews where the nonwhite was directed to different, but not inferior, accommodation).

Things appear better, and indeed in some respects *are* better, for British nonwhites in the mid-1970s as compared with their situation ten years earlier. The race relations climate is more hopeful and there is less overt discrimination. Yet there remain substantial gaps between the groups. Some of these gaps are attributable to disadvantage associated with race. Others suggest the persistence of racial discrimination, in somewhat more subtle form than in the past. Still others reveal the enduring effects of past discrimination.[26] David Smith's *Racial Disadvantage in Britain*, a sober and careful compendium of mid-1970s bad news, summarizes the situation with respect to employment.

> The minority groups are more vulnerable to unemployment than whites; they are concentrated within the lower job levels in a way that cannot be explained by lower academic or job qualifications; within broad categories or jobs they have lower earnings than whites, particularly at the higher end of the job scale; they tend to do shiftwork, which is generally thought to be undesirable, but shiftwork premiums do not raise their earnings above those of whites, because the jobs are intrinsically badly paid; they are concentrated within certain plants, and they have to make about twice as many applications as whites before finding a job.[27]

The situation concerning housing is similarly dispiriting. Nonwhites live in more crowded conditions: nearly 40 percent of nonwhites, as compared with 11 percent of whites, reside in households with two or more persons per bedroom. Their dwellings are older, in worse physical condition, and possess fewer amenities: over half of all Pakistanis, as compared with some 17 percent of whites, live without their own bath, hot water, and inside toilet. Nor do these differences merely reflect income: poor non-whites occupy worse housing than comparably poor whites.[28]

The racial data do not permit an unequivocal appraisal of the policy of inexplicitness, a fact that should occasion no surprise. They do sharpen the focus. The past decade has been marked by some amelioration of relations between races; it is by no means clear how much the tendency to inexplicitness in racial matters contributed to that amelioration. It is also the case that deep inequalities persist; whether these could have been lessened by a more vigorous and directed public policy response is equally uncertain. If we cannot resolve these ultimate policy questions, we can at least view them in a usefully different light by contrasting the American and British policy approaches to race.

Policy Constraint and Policy Choice: Britain and the United States

The circumstances are what render every . . . political scheme beneficial or noxious.[29]

Let us not be Bourbons and let us learn cheaply and vicariously from the experiences of others.[30]

The German poet Heine was once asked where he would most like to be, if the end of the world were declared imminent. England, Heine is said to have replied, because it is always a hundred years behind the times. With race relations, as with doomsday prophesies, Britain is often described as a nation behind the times, by critics less kind than Heine. Inexplicitness, it is argued, signifies nothing more than problem avoidance; it reveals not governmental intelligence or becoming modesty, but an absence of needed resources and a default of imagination. Thus Philippe Nonet and Philip Selznick argue:

> [R]epression occurs when limited resources invite a policy of benign neglect. Confronted with pressing issues of justice or public welfare, the government may seek to avoid commitments and resist demands. New claims are given low priority or brushed aside as illegitimate. Through neglect, the state controls the rise of expectations. It does so partly out of awareness of genuine limits to political and administrative capacity and partly out of fear that frustrated expectations will undermine the foundations of political allegiance and public peace.[31]

Inevitably, it is asserted (and in rather fewer than Heine's hundred years), Britain will be obliged squarely to confront its multiracial reality under circumstances rendered less than auspicious by the policy neglect of the past.

This critique of racial inexplicitness animates a final examination of the policy. The critique presumes, first, that Britain could do things differently if it wished, a proposition properly qualified by those specially British aspects of the racial questions; and, second, that explicitness is itself a good thing, a proposition appropriately tested against the American experience with such an approach.

The Differences Between Countries. The most stunningly obvious facts bearing on the racial situation in the United States and Britain all speak to what is distinctive about each. To note the differences concerning demography, history, and decision-making style is to rehearse the familiar; it is a useful enterprise nonetheless, for these differences help fix the bounds of policy choice.

The nonwhite population of Britain is proportionately far smaller than that of the United States: more than 15 percent of Americans, as compared with some 3 percent of Britons, are nonwhite. Moreover, the major cities of the United States are dominated, at least numerically, by nonwhites, a trend that is increasing; by the mid-1980s, New York, Chicago, St. Louis, Philadelphia, Detroit, Cleveland, Baltimore, Washington, and New Orleans, among other cities, will all be more than half nonwhite. In Britain, by contrast, the nonwhite population remains in all places a decided minority: in no city of any size does it exceed one in eight.

These population differences find their reflection, in exaggerated form, in the primary and secondary schools. In 1970, the ten biggest urban American school systems all enrolled more than 20 percent black students, while four of the ten were majority black.[32] Only six of Britain's more than 500 educational authorities, none of them among the largest, were more than 20 percent nonwhite in 1970, and while there are now more such places, their number does not begin to approach the American situation.

Demography bespeaks policy here. A minority population of 5 or 10 percent can remain invisible, for practical purposes. A minority population that is substantially larger necessarily influences a range of urban policies: it cannot be ignored.

Nor are the nonwhite populations in the United States and Britain readily comparable in terms of background. The largest nonwhite American group is the black community (blacks make up more than three-fifths of the minority population),[33] and while blacks are as heterogeneous as any American ethnic group, they do share a historical and cultural heritage. Not so for the British nonwhites: differences stemming from region of origin (Indian subcontinent or Caribbean), urban or rural origin, and status—differences derived from the country of origin—remain profound. The common experience of America's blacks has strong positive elements, including what may be termed a black culture.[34] The common experience of Britain's nonwhites consists essentially of white Britons' treatment of them; it is, in the main, negative.

These cultural differences between nonwhites in the two nations also have policy significance. One can speak about American blacks with some confidence that one has not thereby created through choice of language a commonality that otherwise does not exist. Not so about Britain's nonwhites, who sometimes seem less a meaningful group or class than a categorical artifact, rather like redheads.

The historical differences between American blacks and British nonwhites are the best known of the distinctions. Blacks came to America involuntarily, more than two centuries ago. They remained slaves until the mid-nineteenth century. Even when free, blacks were subjected to overt discrimination, officially authorized and sanctioned, until the passage of the 1964 Civil Rights Act. They have only begun to participate as formal equals in American political, economic, and social life. Britain's nonwhites enjoyed a very different history. While the West Indies knew slavery in the eighteenth century, the status of nonwhites both in the Indian subcontinent and the Caribbean was not at all similar to that of American blacks.[35] Nonwhites came very late to Britain, and willingly. For some, the nation embodied a valued set of societal ideals; for all, it offered the prospect of economic advancement. Although nonwhites encountered discrimination, especially at the level of privately made policy, never were they subject to official denigration because of their skin color, as was the case in America. John Bull did not learn from Jim Crow.

History too bears on the present. A good deal of America's racial policy, especially policy crafted by the judiciary, takes the sins of the past as its warrant for present-day interventions: past discrimination, as the Supreme Court has stated, is to be eliminated "root and branch."[36] More generally, the shared realization that as a nation America has ill-treated blacks—a realization dramatically brought home to millions of Americans who, in 1963, watched on television as the Birmingham, Alabama, police assaulted peaceful civil rights demonstrations with guard dogs and fire hoses—provided a vital impetus for governmental action. In Britain, there exists no readily detectible residue of social guilt, and policy initiatives with respect to race derive from other sources. The creation of a government agency armed with substantial legal clout to address issues of sex discrimination led the Labour Party to propose enlarging the powers of the agency concerned with racial discrimination almost as a matter of policy symmetry: this, and not a heightened concern for racial inequities, is the commonly advanced explanation for the 1976 Race Relations Act.

A less familiar but at least equally important distinction centers on what for want of a more precise description might be termed the customary style of decision making in the two countries. One aspect of this style relates to the preference for consensual decision making within the British administrative apparatus, touched upon at the outset of the chapter. Yet "style" is intended to convey a broader meaning. American policy decisions are often made directly, as either or propositions, in visible, formal, adversarial settings. The legalist influence prevails, both in the relatively greater American reliance on the judiciary as a problem solver and more pervasively in the emulation of the judicial approach in nonjudicial settings. The British norms are, by decided contrast, nonconfrontational, nonformal, and nonlegal.

This distinction pertains generally to social welfare policy. Lawlike behavior—including recourse to the adversarial process and clear, potentially precedent-making outcomes—is far more in evidence in the United States than in Britain.[37] The distinction applies with special force to the issue of race relations, which in America has largely been conceptualized in terms of rules, legal do's and don'ts.[38] The United States has grown accustomed to this approach during the past quarter-century. It took an authoritative judicial determination of constitutional obligation with respect to race in the school segregation cases, amplified and enforced by congressional and executive action under the 1964 Civil Rights Act, to make nondiscrimination national policy.

Even as the meaning of nondiscrimination in the United States has expanded and grown consequently less clear, the primary enforcers remain the judiciary and administrative agencies, acting not as persuasive instrumentalities but rather as wielders of positive law. The aim of federal administrative agency inquiries into allegations of employment discrimination, for example, is to determine the facts and apply the relevant rule of law, an objective drawn from judicial, not political or administrative, experience. The means deployed by the agency to achieve its ends also derive from the judiciary. In the racial realm, American administrative practice does not rely on suasion or sanctionless pressure—"jawboning," as it is termed in the context of wage and price regulation. Nor does the authorizing legislation permit administrative agencies to make use of policy designs particularly appropriate for agency (as opposed to court) administration, such as taxing discriminatory behavior or offering incentives to encourage nondiscriminatory behavior. The technique employed, denial of federal funds, is the administrative equivalent to a judicially imposed penalty.

This legalist approach has reconfigured racial politics in America. It has rendered the legal process nothing less than an alternative mode of political participation for those previously victimized by discrimination, an end-run around the often frustratingly slow, compromise-prone, majoritarian political system.

The treatment of race and schooling illustrates these general propositions. For the past decade, the management of antidiscrimination efforts with respect to schools has been almost exclusively the province of American courts. Desegregation, the policy-relevant task, has become a matter of rule-mindedness, obedience to (or defiance of) court decisions. School districts that obey the law by not discriminating against black students are impervious to legal challenge. Conversely, those that break the rules suffer reprimand and are ordered to behave differently; resistance brings judicial contempt citations, more precise orders, or loss of federal funds. In such instances, the imposed remedy is supposed both to secure the legal rights of blacks and to punish official wrongdoing.

The legalist approach came into prominence during the 1960s, as a response to necessity. It is difficult to imagine how the blatantly racist subterfuges practiced by Southern school districts during that era might have been undone differently. That approach has persisted and become bureaucratized in the 1970s, under circumstances in which neither legal nor moral right and wrong are so clear cut. The causes of present-day segregation are more murky; the likelihood of undoing segregation by decree seems remote; even the desirability of making the attempt, through massive changes in educational systems, is subject to question.

Such altered circumstances might be thought properly to have given rise to a different and less legalist stance. As Supreme Court Justice Byron White has noted:

> The [court's] task is not to devise a system of pains and penalties to punish constitutional violations brought to light. Rather, it is to desegregate an *educational* system in which the races have been kept apart, without at the same time, losing sight of the central *educational* function of the schools.[39]

Justice White's statement was offered in dissent, in a case in which the Supreme Court distinguished desegregation in law from desegregation in fact, suggesting that the former—all that the constitution required—was achievable within Detroit, an 80 percent black school district. The Supreme Court has continued to preserve the essentially legalist cast of the question, linking the scope of court-ordered desegregation with fault finding by the judiciary.[40] Policy considerations, including the desirability of inherently less confrontationist approaches to the issue, have consistently been given short shrift in the Court's treatment of school segregation.

So too with other knotty questions concerning race, ethnicity, and schooling: issues of policy have been converted into questions of formal legal right, whether by court decision, as with the non-English-speaking child's entitlement to bilingual instruction,[41] or administrative ruling, as with the permissibility of exclusively minority schools chosen by minority students.[42] Even the "correctness" of textbook depiction of minority students becomes the subject of a state law, rather than an exchange between publishers and educators.

In this regard, the British situation is almost wholly different. The considerably greater reticence of the British judiciary is partly attributable to the absolute supremacy of Parliament and the unavailability of judicial review of parliamentary actions on constitutional grounds.[43] But the difference between the two systems is not just structural. Even where the propriety of judicial review is unquestioned, as in passing on alleged statutory violations, the inclination of the British courts is to narrow the issue at hand, minimizing its policy implications: this has certainly been true with respect to those cases decided under the race relations legislation.[44]

Nor do British administrative agencies behave as if they were courts. DES has not been inclined to adopt lawlike modes of responding to allegations of racial discrimination even when authorized to do so, as under the 1976 Race Relations Act. Whether the issue be the asserted overrepresentation of nonwhites in classes for the retarded, the permissibility of dress and conduct requirements that affect nonwhites with special force, or the appropriateness of native language instruction in basic subjects, DES's tendency has been to rely upon informal inquiry and agreed-upon *ad hoc* solutions, not definitive statements of right.[45]

These differences of decisional style obviously and directly affect policy choices. The distinction between the adversarial and legalist, on the one hand, the nonconfrontationist and nonformal on the other, is significant in its own right. It also shapes the range of substantive policies available in each country.

The Possibility of Policy Learning: On Doing Good by Doing Little.

The profound differences between the racial situation in Britain and in the United States, and the equally vital differences in the policy environment in which race gets considered, tell only part of the policy story. Exclusively to stress the variations between the two nations ignores nascent common themes, and the consequent possibility of real policy learning.

Unlike judicial decision making, which instinctively looks to the past for guidance, policy making in the executive and legislative branches tends to ahistoricism. What matters—or, at least, matters most—is the present. With respect to racial issues, the present, for America and Britain, reveals far more likenesses than has the past.

Although discrimination in the United States persists, it no longer enjoys the sanction of law: as in Britain, discrimination has become more a furtive and private, and not an open and public matter. Racial discrimination in America now seems of less policy moment than even a decade ago. What appears newly significant is disadvantage more nebulously linked to race, and more clearly tied to economic circumstance.

As the distinguished black sociologist William Julius Wilson comments: "The systematic efforts of whites to suppress blacks . . . [h]owever determinative . . . for the previous efforts of the black people to achieve racial equality . . . do not provide a meaningful explanation of the life chances of black Americans today." In the modern industrial era, particularly within the past ten years, Wilson reports "*progressive transition from racial inequalities to class inequalities*." Talented, highly educated blacks are experiencing unprecedented job opportunities, both because of changes in the economy and governmental support: for them, nondiscrimination has become a reality. None of this has aided the poorly trained inner city blacks who, together with their undereducated white counterparts, are seemingly fated to endure permanent marginal economic and social status. Wilson does not deny the persistence of "racial antagonism in the sociopolitical order," but minimizes its significance. Such antagonism, he asserts, has far less effect on individual or group access to those opportunities and resources that are centrally important for life survival than antagonism in the economic sector.[46]

By focusing on the primary of economic rather than racial inequality, Wilson's assessment (much like that earlier advanced by Daniel Moynihan)[47] resembles British postwar social policy thought more than American analyses, undertaken a decade ago, which spoke hyperbolically of the emergence of racially separate and unequal nations.[48] Wilson's position finds some support in other recent scholarly work, as well as in less racially specific undertakings within the American black community. A leading civil rights organization, for example, has supported the oil industry's position concerning price deregulation on the grounds that deregulation would strengthen the economy by reducing unemployment; that consequence would, if realized, be of real but only indirect benefit to blacks. Black politicians increasingly stress the importance of literacy and numeracy, not racial identity, as critical to the educational success of black students, even as black academics point out predominantly black schools which, by stressing discipline, have produced a record of solid academic performance.[49] In increasing numbers and with relatively little fuss, affluent blacks are moving into previously all-white suburbs; there are as many blacks in Fairfax County, Virginia, a suburb of Washington, D.C., as in the city of Pittsburgh.

These data constitute fragments, shreds of evidence and not proof of a paradigmatic shift with respect to race. They need to be qualified by the realization that in certain spheres, such as access to housing, widespread racial discrimination does persist.[50] It is nonetheless the case that white Americans, when surveyed, overwhelmingly believe that race *per se* has a diminishing impact on one's life chances. Whites recognize that, as a group, blacks are worse off than they are. They do not, however, attribute this fact primarily to racial discrimination. "[Whites] sympathize with blacks over past mistreatment and are increasingly aware of the continuing vestiges of discrimination. At the same time, they deeply resent what they perceive as the unwillingness of many blacks to live by the standards of middle-class America." The white majority, while supportive of government aid to disadvantaged groups intended "to help [them] catch up to the standards of competition set by the larger society,"[51] is strongly disapproving of preferential treatment. Blacks too endorse a color-blind, merit-based standard over a racially explicit standard that favors blacks, although by a smaller margin. Among the majority, racial inexplicitness, in the form of compensation to those needing special help, commands enthusiasm. Racial explicitness, at least with respect to hiring and university admissions, provokes hostility.

American debates over vital racial policy issues also reveal an interest in remedies less racially explicit than has been the policy rule since the 1954 segregation cases.

Two familiar examples, court-ordered busing and racially preferential treatment, illustrate the proposition.

The busing of schoolchildren to achieve something approaching racial balance has been ordered by federal courts, ostensibly to undo the effects of deliberate and unconstitutional segregation. When the Supreme Court approved this technique, it was in the context of dismantling segregation in a school district that, fifteen years earlier, had maintained separate black and white schools.[52] The busing of substantial numbers of children on racial grounds has subsequently been required in Northern school districts found to have "deliberately" isolated black and white schoolchildren,[53] despite the fact that this separation could not be attributed to formal legal mandate.

Identifying deliberate segregation in the North is a factually and legally subtler proposition than in the South. It requires investigation of, among other things, the bases for student assignment, the drawing of school attendance zone boundaries, and the placement of black and white teachers in ways assertedly intended to signal the fact that a particular school is "black" or "white." It is also a more disputed proposition: while no one doubted that Atlanta or Charlotte-Meckenburg, North Carolina, had once parcelled out students on racial lines, there were grave doubts that San Francisco or Minneapolis had behaved similarly, whatever findings a court might make in these cases.[54]

As the definition of "deliberate"—and hence proscribable—segregation has broadened, the wrong has grown harder to comprehend. Moreover, the nexus between the alleged discrimination and the sweeping remedy of reassigning students throughout a city's public school system appears remote, at least to the popular mind, and hence arbitrary. This judicially crafted development has provoked spirited critiques rooted in concern for educational choice,[55] as well as for the constitutionally appropriate allocation of power between the political and judicial branches of the federal government. Both sources of concern respond to a substantive unhappiness with an explicitly racial policy, the busing of schoolchildren.

Even more dramatic are the divisions among liberal Americans, once united in the civil rights coalition, over the wisdom of explicitly preferential treatment of nonwhites.[56] On one side stand those who insist that the appropriate measure of nondiscrimination is full partnership in the social, political, and economic order; that full partnership can be defined only in outcome terms, as proportionate participation; that past discrimination gives normative warrant for this remedy; that less rigorous measures are unresponsive to the demand for equality; and that, at least as a temporary expedient where such nominally neutral criteria as merit testing do not achieve this result, racial preference in the form of quotas is appropriate. On the other side stand those who believe that the constitution forbids the singling out of racial groups for any purpose, and who are consequently opposed to reliance on race as a policy criterion even for ostensibly good causes, especially where others, themselves innocent of any wrongdoing, are hurt as a result.

Unlike the historic efforts to combat discrimination in the United States, the dispute over preferential treatment cannot be depicted as a struggle between good and evil; it is rather a choice between two concepts of good. As British historian J. R. Pole writes: "Broad policies of equalization implemented for the benefit of groups whose grievances and deprivations were felt to give their individual members special claims on the community clash with the equally fundamental rights of other individuals . . . whose rights were derived from the same sources and ascertained by the same methods of inquiry."[57] Nor does this dispute pit proponents of equality against advocates of inequality. Instead, the principled partisans in this fray each advance a definition of equality, one group- and the other individual-centered, one outcome- and the other process-oriented, one insisting upon racial explicitness and the other resistant to using race as a predicate for special treatment.

Justice Powell's opinion in *University of California v. Bakke*,[58] the first Supreme Court decision to address the issue of preferential treatment, is acutely attentive to these normative complexities. In permitting universities to take a student's race into account in the admissions process while barring reliance on formal racial quotas, the Court insists upon inexplicitness as the constitutionally mandated policy choice. *Bakke* suggests a constitutional value in not being too race-specific.

The point of these illustrations is not that the wisdom of court-ordered busing and the permissibility of preferential treatment can or should be resolved by mechanical reference to the principle of racial inexplicitness. The issues are far too complex, the values at tension far too deep for that. It is rather that, in recognizing that racial questions are no longer the matters of simple justice that they once were,[59] and that their explicit resolution is not necessarily the appropriate course, America may be moving closer to the long-standing British position.

The Policy Challenge

In the racial realm, Britain and the United States confront distinct but complementary policy challenges. The American policy task, succinctly stated, is to link a well-developed constitutional understanding of racial fairness with the emerging possibility of a sense of justice at once more finely tuned and *ad hoc*, less clearly defined and generalizable, that can emerge politically in particular situations.

Several factors—normative, political, and institutional—suggest how difficult it will be to achieve this objective. It may be argued—indeed, in the context of the Moynihan memorandum, was argued—that inexplicitness is a morally bankrupt response to America's history of discrimination. The force of this position is undoubted, but the question remains: Can policy serve as a self-fulfilling prophecy in this realm? Can the nation render race of less actual moment by minimizing its policy significance—even against the weight of historical circumstance? At a different level, in the United States, racial politics, particularly at the state and local levels, has most frequently been deployed to frustrate legitimate minority aspirations. Whether it can give a fuller reckoning to those aspirations is untested. The American judiciary has with rare exception eschewed the passive virtues inherent in avoiding decisions. It has preferred clarity to compromise, principle to politics. Can one imagine the issue of busing or preferential treatment ultimately being resolved by other than a Supreme Court decision?

For Britain, with whose policies we are primarily concerned, the situation is quite different. The need, briefly put, is to couple the considerable virtues of inexplicitness with both a greater willingness to incorporate nonwhite groups into the relevant decision-making and consultative apparatuses, and a recognition that discrimination—unequal treatment based on race—deserves more serious public policy attention than it has thus far received.

Discrimination ought to be anathema in a country that historically has placed such a high value on personal liberty. Nondiscrimination represents the legal embodiment of respect for the individual, the formal guarantee that group identity will not denigrate the person. Nondiscrimination involves undoing rules or practices that are explicitly disadvantaging. As the 1976 Race Relations Act recognizes, it also requires that attention be paid to practices which, while not overtly racial, nonetheless operate to disadvantage racial minorities without adequate justification. This undertaking does not equate differences between the minority and majority as necessarily disadvantaging. It does suggest the appropriateness of sensitive appraisal of the nature and the invidiousness of those differences. Such an inquiry—which the newly authorized collection of racial data can only aid—is meant to focus attention on unintended intolerance: behavior which thoughtlessly injures is often of this variety.

To a considerable extent, the condition in which British nonwhites find themselves is attributable not to racial discrimination, but to disadvantage less directly linked to race. How to deal with such disadvantage as a policy matter is most problematic. Some response may well be called for, but race-specific remedies do not necessarily make sense. Pakistanis and Indians, to cite one instance, often have large families, and hence need larger houses than the housing authorities typically have available; that is one reason why they have tended to purchase housing of inferior quality.[60] But is it family size, or the link between Asians and family size, on which policy is properly focused? West Indian children, to note another example, fare less well in school than whites, even those of comparable social class backgrounds; but it neither follows that the causes of poor performance are race-specific, nor that the tools of policy intervention are sufficiently refined to permit an effective race-specific remedy. What one would do to improve West Indian achievement that would not work as well for the London Cockney is not clear; in this context, the proposed broadening of the terms of the grants programs designed to aid nonwhites is sensible.

On occasion, it makes good sense to attend to the racial dimension of a policy problem, as by bringing nonwhites and whites together, at least so long as attention is not focused on the undertaking. That practice, familiar in the annals of both housing and schooling, is hard to defend logically; it is nonetheless right. If the ultimate end of public policy is to minimize the imposed salience of race while freeing individuals to choose for themselves what to make of their race, how better to proceed than to encourage integrated schools and housing estates and factories? The teachers in Ealing forgot that the students who had been bused into their schools were nonwhite immigrants: what clearer measure of the success of dispersal could there be?[61] On numerous occasions, British officials have to choose between courses of action, one of whose consequences is to segregate or mix the races. In such circumstances—as for instance in recruitment for government-run industry or in selecting sites for housing estates and new schools—the preference for racial mixing as a natural component of policy is appropriate. Only when official preference for integration is used to override the expressed desire of nonwhites to remain a coherent and separate group does racial specificity become troubling.

This treatment of discrimination and disadvantage speaks to the substantive questions raised by those in Britain who propose race-specific policies. If it does not fully meet the issue, it at least reveals that racial inexplicitness need not imply inattentiveness. Those concerned about the lack of nonwhite participation in shaping British race policy raise issues of a quite different order. Insofar as the message conveyed is that not enough nonwhite voices get heard in government, the criticism is fair enough. For a bureaucracy that seemingly consults with everyone, discussions with particular groups within the nonwhite community would not be out of order. When the matter is framed in terms of constituency and representation, however, it assumes an altogether more troubling shape. To reach decisions by consensus among constituencies organized along ethnic lines is to call into being a society very different from one endeavoring to maintain pluralism and individualism in delicate balance.

These points have specific bearing on British educational policy, the focus of the inquiry. The nondiscrimination principle suggests that, at the least, claims by nonwhites who have been victimized on account of race receive an attentive hearing; and that, beyond this, certain practices that appear to disadvantage nonwhites as a group—disproportionate representation of nonwhites in classes for the educationally subnormal, for example—be subject to careful review. Uniquely among governmental departments, under the 1976 Race Relations Act DES has the specific authority to attend to such matters before they are brought to the courts. It ought to use that power wisely, in order to keep these matters from becoming tangled in legalisms.[62]

The British educational system needs also to celebrate a diversity of interests among the current generation of students, to recognize and attend to the richness in variety. It is not cultural condescension to note that the Sikhs (and, for that matter, the Scots) have a bountiful heritage which, quite like the Norman conquest, is (or is becoming) part and parcel of British "lore and culture." Accommodation of diversity implies also that greater attention be paid to the principle of family choice with respect to schooling that undergirds the 1944 Education Act; and this, not just with respect to the wishes of nonwhites. It further implies that, within the state system, efforts be made to broaden the instructional regime consistent with the interests and inclinations of those charged with managing and teaching in the schools. That undertaking calls not for an abandonment of standards of excellence but rather for harnessing new (or newly relevant) resources to enduring educational purposes. The paths to be avoided are, on the one hand, a descent into mindless multiculturalism and, on the other, a determined effort to preserve the past for the sake of preservation.[63] It is in fusing what deserves to endure with the contributions of the present that the educational system will most effectively respond to issues of race.

This is all unspecific: intentionally so. Beyond effectively assuring nondiscrimination, particular matters are probably best resolved in the particular, not by general pronouncement. What matters most is the analytic framework which shapes particular resolutions. Philip Mason states it well.

> What we have to do—and here by "we" I mean Britain—is to direct our whole educational system toward the treatment of other groups and people as autonomous persons with their own values and yet achieve this within a system of authority and a unity of values. But it must be an adult system of values, that is, one which each constituent accepts as its own. At the same time, there is the insoluble dilemma that, violent as is our need, we cannot literally "direct" our system of education into any channel without doing violence to our own beliefs about intellectual freedom.[64]

This is an immensely difficult enterprise, calling for exquisite sensitivity and command for nuance. It also represents an aspiration, not a policy prescription. The question remains: Can Britain preserve the considerable benefits of inexplicitness, even as it safeguards the nondiscrimination principle and the idea of tolerance underlying it?[65]

The ultimate hope for both Britain and the United States is much the same. What is wanted in the racial realm is a public policy that neither becomes officious intermeddling nor degenerates into mere neglect, with the result that race eventually ceases to be a policy problem. As to the likelihood of that ultimately occurring in either nation, it is far too soon even to hazard predictions.

Notes

For book references, the number following the title refers to the page or pages quoted. For journal article references, the number preceding a journal title refers to the volume; the number following the journal title refers to the beginning page of the article. The year is in parentheses.

one
A British Dilemma: Public Policy, Private Policy, and Race

1. Local educational authorities are the British equivalent of American school districts.
2. See Catherine Jones, *Immigration and Social Policy in Britain* (London: Tavistock, 1977).
3. 347 U.S. 483 (1954).
4. These questions have been thoroughly dissected. In the schools context, see Mark Yudof, "Equal Educational Opportunity and the Courts" 51 *Texas Law Review* 411 (1973), and Frank Goodman, "De Facto School Desegregation: A Constitutional and Empirical Analysis" 60 *California Law Review* 275 (1972). See generally Owen Fiss, "Groups and the Equal Protection Clause" 5 *Philosophy and Public Affairs* 107 (1976).
5. On preferential treatment, see Robert O'Neil, *Discrimination Against Discrimination: Preferential Admission in the DeFunis Case* (Bloomington: Indiana University Press, 1975); Allan Sindler, *Bakke, DeFunis, and Minority Admissions: The Quest for Equal Opportunity* (New York: Longman, 1978).
6. Nicholas Deakin, *Colour, Citizenship, and British Society* 22 (London: Panther, 1970).
7. John Ruskin, *A Joy For Ever* 100, quoted in V. G. Kiernan, *The Lords of Human Kind* 321 (London: Weidenfeld and Nicholson, 1969).
8. I shall use the terms *racial minority* and *nonwhite* to describe those who migrated to Britain from the Caribbean,

the Indian subcontinent, and Africa, and who were not themselves of British stock. The variety of terms deployed to describe this group is extensive: *coloured*, *New Commonwealth Immigrant*, *black* have all enjoyed currency, and the choice among these is controversial. See text at note 83, *infra*.

9. Deakin, *supra* note 6, at 25.
10. Some of the migration from India and Pakistan is attributable to the hardship borne by particular religious and community groups who found themselves on the "wrong" side of the border between the two new countries fashioned at the time of independence. In that sense, Britain's responsibility for the immigrants is directly traceable to its own actions. The dual citizenship provision may also have been adopted to protect the interests of white colonials—Anglo-Indians, for instance—who might subsequently want to return to Britain.
11. J. R. Pole, *The Pursuit of Equality in American History* 341 (Berkeley and Los Angeles: University of California Press, 1978).
12. Philip Mason, *Prospero's Magic: Some Thoughts on Class and Race* 39 (London: Oxford University Press, 1962). In *Destiny,* a widely acclaimed play linking racial hatred and the demise of Empire, Rudyard Kipling's "The Beginnings" is quoted in this context:

> It was not part of their blood,
> It came to them very late
> With long arrears to make good,
> When the English began to hate.
>
> They were not easily moved,
> They were icy-willing to wait
> Till every count should be proved,
> Ere the English began to hate.
>
> Their voices were even and low,
> Their eyes were level and straight.
> There was neither sign nor show,
> When the English began to hate.
>
> It was not preached to the crow,
> It was not taught by the State.
> No man spoke it aloud,
> When the English began to hate.

It was not suddenly bred,
  It will not swiftly abate,
Through the chill years ahead,
  When Time shall count from the date
  That the English began to hate.

Verse 677 (Garden City, N.Y.: Doubleday, Doran, 1942).

13. Anthony Lester and Geoffrey Bindman, *Race and Law in Great Britain* 13 (Cambridge, Mass.: Harvard University Press, 1972).
14. Both Mason, *supra* note 12, and Ann Dummett, *A Portrait of English Racism* (Harmondsworth: Penguin, 1972), discuss the relationships between race and class.
15. See e.g., E. G. B. Rose, et al., *Colour and Citizenship* (London: Oxford University Press, 1969); David Smith, *Racial Disadvantage in Britain* (Harmondsworth: Pelican, 1977); Catherine Jones, *supra* note 2; Ben Heineman, Jr., *The Politics of the Powerless* (London: Oxford University Press, 1972); Ira Katznelson, *Black Men, White Cities: Race Politics and Migration in the United States 1900–30 and Britain 1948–68* (London: Oxford University Press, 1968); G. C. K. Peach, *West Indian Migration to Britain: A Social Geography* (London: Oxford University Press, 1968); Sheila Patterson, *Immigration and Race Relations in Britain, 1960–67* (London: Oxford University Press, 1969); John Rex and Robert Moore, *Race, Community and Conflict* (London: Oxford University Press, 1967); Michael Banton, *Race Relations* (London: Tavistock, 1967).
16. Quoted in Deakin, *supra* note 6, at 109.
17. *Id.* at 47. The McCarran Act, which fixed American immigration policy, discriminated against British subjects of African descent and thus deflected West Indian migrants toward Britain.
18. David Smith, *supra* note 15, at 21.
19. See, e.g., the survey results reported in Daniel Lawrence, *Black Migrants: White Natives* (London: Cambridge University Press, 1974).
20. Quoted in Deakin, *supra* note 6, at 283.
21. Jones, *supra* note 2, at 132–133.
22. The observation made by Oxford historian Goldwin Smith in 1878, is quoted in Christine Bolt, *Victorian Attitudes to Race* 214 (London: Routledge and Kegan Paul, 1971).
23. Dipak Nandy, "Foreword" to Julia McNeal and Margaret Rogers, *The Multi-Racial School* (Harmondsworth: Penguin, 1971).

24. A. Sivanandan, "Race, Class and the State: The Black Experience in Britain," 17 *Race and Class* 347 (1976).
25. See generally Lawrence, *supra* note 19, and Katznelson, *supra* note 15.
26. 264 H.L. Deb. col 166, 10 March 1965.
27. Quoted in Dummett, *supra* note 14, at 190.
28. Goldwin Smith, *supra* note 22.
29. Quoted in Thomas Metcalf, *The Aftermath of Revolt: India 1857–1870* 292 (Princeton: Princeton University Press, 1964). See generally D. K. Fieldhouse, *The Colonial Empires* (London: Weidenfeld and Nicolson, 1966).
30. E. M. Forster, *A Passage to India* 39 (London: J. M. Dent, 1957 ed.).
31. James Bryce, 1 *Studies in History and Jurisprudence* 980 (New York: Oxford University Press, 1901).
32. On race and paternalism in America, see Eugene Genovese, *Roll, Jordan, Roll: The World The Slaves Made* (New York: Pantheon, 1974).
33. Quoted in Bolt, *supra* note 22, at 77.
34. Mason, *supra* note 14, at 95.
35. *Id.*
36. Forster, *supra* note 30, at 32.
37. W. Collins, *Jamaican Migrant* 116 (London: Routledge and Kegan Paul, 1965). Since it has become unfashionable in some circles to admit feelings of superiority, these survey findings probably understate the extent to which the attitude of superiority prevails.
38. Deakin, *supra* note 6, at 325.
39. Michael Banton, *White and Coloured* (London: Cape, 1959).
40. Deakin, *supra* note 6, at 326.
41. See Alan Marsh, "Who Hates the Blacks?" *New Society* 649 (23 September 1976).
42. Dummett, *supra* note 14, at 14.
43. Gunnar Myrdal, 1 *An American Dilemma* 89 (New York: Harper and Row, 1967 ed.) (italics in original).
44. J. R. Pole, *supra* note 11, at 325–326. See also W. J Cash, *The Mind of the South* (New York: Random House, 1941); Charles Silberman, *Crisis in Black and White* (New York: Random House, 1964); C. Vann Woodward, *The Strange Career of Jim Crow* (New York: Oxford University Press, 1966).
45. Dummett, *supra* note 13, at 88.
46. R. V. Hunt and others, *Times Law Report,* 16 September 1958.
47. *The Economist* 506, col. 1 (7 August 1965).

48. Quoted in Deakin, *supra* note 6, at 106.
49. *Id.* at 337.
50. *Id.* at 112.
51. Jones, *supra* note 2, at 147.
52. See Dipak Nandy, "An Illusion of Competence," in Anthony Lester and Nicholas Deakin, eds., *Racial Equality* (London: Fabian Society, 1967).
53. Michael Hill and Ruth Issacharoff, *Community Action and Race Relations* (London: Oxford University Press, 1971); Chris Mullard, *Black Britain* (London: George Allen and Unwin, 1973).
54. A commissioned inquiry into the working of American civil rights law was one of the bases for the 1968 British legislation. See Harry Street, Geoffrey Howe, and Geoffrey Bindman, *Report on Anti-Discrimination Legislation* (London: Political and Economic Planning, 1967).
55. The Race Relations Board data are drawn from *Report of the Race Relations Board*: January 1975–June 1976 (London: HMSO, 1976). By contrast, 54,074 allegations of discrimination were filed in fiscal year 1976 with the Equal Employment Opportunity Commission, the American agency which deals with employment discrimination alone. The number of discrimination complaints lodged with all American agencies, and cases filed in court, would be many times higher.
56. *London Borough of Ealing v. Race Relations Board* [1972] 1 All E.R. 105.
57. Alexis de Tocqueville, 1 *Democracy in America* 280 (New York: Knopf, 1951).
58. *U.S. v. Carolene Products Co.,* 304 U.S. 144, 152 n. 4 (1938).
59. *Somerset v. Stewart,* 98 English Reports 499 (1772); *The Slave, Grace,* 166 English Reports 179 (1827).
60. Jones, *supra* note 2, at 51.
61. Lawrence, *supra* note 19, at 192.
62. Jones, *supra* note 2, at 176–177.
63. *Id.*
64. *Id.* at 175.
65. Smith, *supra* note 15, at 322.
66. Jones, *supra* note 2, at 193.
67. See generally Nathan Glazer, *Affirmative Discrimination* (New York: Basic Books, 1975).
68. The recounting of social service agencies' response is drawn from Jones, *supra* note 2, at 184–255.
69. *Id.* at 229.

70. This is indeed the case. See Smith, *supra* note 15, at 243–284.
71. Jones, *supra* note 2, at 243.
72. J. David Greenstone and Paul E. Peterson, *Race and Authority in Urban Politics: Community Participation and the War on Poverty* (Chicago: University of Chicago Press, 1976).
73. Quoted in Bolt, *supra* note 22, at 216–217.
74. Quoted in Deakin, *supra* note 6, at 287.
75. *Id.* at 288.
76. Gordon Lewis, "Race Relations in Britain: A View From the Caribbean," *Race Today* (July 1969).
77. See, e.g., Jeff Crawford, "Integration or Independence: A Strategy for Black Groups," *Race Today* (January 1972).
78. See Lawrence, *supra* note 19, at 35.
79. Forster, *supra* note 30, at 218.
80. See Chapter Four, *infra*.
81. See generally Heineman, *supra* note 15.
82. See A. Sivanandan, "Race, Class and Power: An Outline for Study," 14 *Race* 383 (1973).
83. Harold Isaacs, in "Basic Group Identity: The Idols of the Tribe," in Nathan Glazer and Daniel Moynihan, eds., *Ethnicity* 29, 48–49 (Cambridge, Mass.: Harvard University Press, 1975), speaks of these disputes over the "proper" label for an ethnic group as "terminological ironies and curiosities . . . [a way] to give substance and usage to the [sought-after] national identity." Substitute "ethnic" for "national" and the observation nicely applies to the nonwhite groups in Britain.

two
The Evolution of British Race and Schooling Policy

1. For histories of nineteenth- and twentieth-century British education, see David Wardle, *English Popular Education 1780–1970* (Cambridge: Cambridge University Press, 1970); G. A. N. Lowndes, *The Silent Social Revolution* (London: Oxford University Press, 1937); W. O. Lester Smith, *To Whom Do Schools Belong*? (Oxford: Blackwell, 1946). David Rubenstein and Brian Simons, *The Evolution of the Comprehensive School, 1926–1966* (London: Routledge and

Kegan Paul; New York: Humanities Press, 1969) directly takes up the issue of inequality with which this discussion is primarily concerned.

2. Quoted in Wardle, *supra* note 1, at 26.
3. *Id.* at 25. Both statements were made in the years just preceding passage of the 1870 Education Act.
4. C. E. Trevalyan, *On the Education of the People of India* (1838), quoted in Thomas Metcalf, *The Aftermath of Revolt: India 1857–1870* 14 (Princeton: Princeton University Press, 1964).
5. *Id.* at 133 (quoting Lord William Bentinck, Governor General of India, 1828–1835).
6. Quoted in Rubenstein and Simon, *supra* note 1, at 4.
7. Quoted in Lester Smith, *supra* note 1, at 195.
8. Rubenstein and Simon, *supra* note 1, at 21.
9. H. C. Dent, *Change in English Education* 14 (London: University of London Press, 1942).
10. Lester Smith, *supra* note 1, at 195.
11. Consultative Committee to the Board of Education, *The Education of the Adolescent* 78 (London: HMSO, 1926) (The Hadow Report).
12. Secondary School Examinations Council, *Curriculum and Examinations in Secondary School* 2–3 (London: HMSO 1943) (The Norwood Report).
13. S. J. Curtis, *Education in Britain Since 1900* 144 (London: Dakers, 1952).
14. Quoted in Michael Parkinson, *The Labour Party and the Organization of Secondary Education 1918–1969* 57 (London: Routledge and Kegan Paul, 1970).
15. See Jean Floud and A. H. Halsey, *Social Class and Educational Opportunity* (London: Heineman, 1956).
16. Rubenstein and Simon, *supra* note 1, at 85–88.
17. Wardle, *supra* note 1, at 141–142.
18. Quoted in Maurice Kogan, *Educational Policy-Making* 219–220 (London: George Allen and Unwin, 1975).
19. Quoted in Rubenstein and Simon, *supra* note 1, at 70–71.
20. General treatments of educational policy making during the relevant period, for example, Kogan *supra* note 18, do not even make reference to the education of nonwhites as an issue. The expansion of the higher education system was a second critical policy issue during the 1960s. See Kogan at 185–217.
21. Statistics concerning the numbers and concentration of nonwhite students are drawn from the Department of Edu-

cation's annual publication, *Statistics of Education* (London: HMSO) and from H. E. R. Townsend, *Immigrants in England: The LEA Response* (Slough: National Foundation for Educational Research, 1971). The literature concerning the education of nonwhites in Britain is voluminous. In addition to works cited elsewhere in these notes, see, e.g., Nicholas Hawkes, *Immigrant Children in British Schools* (London: Pall Mall, 1966); Gordon Bowker, *The Education of Coloured Immigrant Children* (London: Longmans, 1968); and Christopher Bagley, *Race Relations and Education* (London: Routledge and Kegan Paul, 1974).

22. See generally David McKay, *Housing and Race in Industrial Society* (London: Croon Helm, 1977).
23. See Martin G. Walker, *The National Front* (London: Fontana, 1977). The National Front is more concerned about "repatriating" the immigrants—sending them back to their country of origin—than with their treatment while in Britain.
24. Christopher Bagley and Gaiendra K. Verma, "Inter-Ethnic Attitudes and Behavior in British Multi-Racial Schools," in Christopher Bagley and Gaiendra K. Verma, eds., *Race and Education Across Cultures* 258, 267–269 (London: Heineman, 1975).
25. H. E. R. Townsend and E. M. Brittan, *Organization in Multiracial Schools* (Slough: National Foundation for Educational Research, 1972).
26. Alan Little, "The Performance of Children from Ethnic Minority Backgrounds in Primary Schools," 1 *Oxford Review of Education* 117 (1975).
27. For a polemic on the subject, see Bernard Coard, *How the West Indian Child Is Made Educationally Subnormal in the British School System* (London: New Beacon, 1971).
28. See Anthony Lester and Geoffrey Bindman, *Race and Law in Great Britain* (Cambridge, Mass.: Harvard University Press, 1971); Ian Macdonald, *Race Relations—the New Law* (London: Butterworths, 1978).
29. *The Problems of Coloured School Leavers* (London: HMSO, 1969); *Education* (London: HMSO, 1973); *The West Indian Community* (London: HMSO, 1977).
30. The possibility of "intentional" segregation is not in fact incredible. In one section of London, a largely nonwhite school was said to have been kept open, in the face of declining enrollments in the area, in order to keep the minority (in this case, Bangladeshi) students in one school.

Elsewhere, the proximity of largely nonwhite and all-white schools gives rise to suspicions of gerrymandering.

31. The policy of dispersing or busing only nonwhite students, as engaged in by the outer London borough of Ealing, was challenged in court by the Race Relations Board as a violation of the 1968 Race Relations Act. The 1976 Race Relations Act permits race-specific treatment to serve the "special needs" of minorities. See Chapter Three for a thorough discussion.
32. Nathan Glazer, *Affirmative Discrimination* 129 (New York: Basic Books, 1975).
33. For an analysis of British government responses to each of these immigrant groups, see Catherine Jones, *Immigration and Social Policy in Britain* (London: Tavistock, 1977). Interestingly enough, at the turn of the century, the British schools were willing to adapt their curriculum to the needs of the Jewish community, something they were less willing to do with respect to minorities. *Id.* at 103–109.
34. *English for Immigrants*, Ministry of Education pamphlet No. 43 (London: HMSO, 1963).
35. *The Education of Immigrants*, Education Survey 13 (London: HMSO, 1971).
36. *The Continuing Needs of Immigrants*, Education Survey 14 (London: HMSO, 1972).
37. The development of these programs is recounted in Nicholas Deakin, *Colour, Citizenship and British Society* 177–183 (London: Panther, 1970). Current expenditure data, here and elsewhere in the chapter, were provided by John Lyttle, advisor to Shirley Williams, Secretary of State for DES.
38. See H. E. R. Townsend, *supra* note 21, *passim*.
39. Community Relations Commission, "Funding Multi-Racial Education: A National Strategy" (unpublished paper, 1976).
40. *Id.*
41. H. E. R. Townsend, *supra* note 21, at 38.
42. Among the co-signatories of "Funding Multi-Racial Education: A National Strategy," *supra* note 39, which called for substantial increases in national expenditures, was the Chief Education Officer of Brent, an outer London borough which claimed only 6.87 pounds of Local Government Act funds per pupil.
43. See the presentation of the Community Relations Commission to the Select Committee on Race Relations and Immigration, *The West Indian Community, supra* note 29, at 525.
44. *Second Report by the Commonwealth Immigrants Advisory*

Council (Cmnd.2266) (London: HMSO, 1964). For a discussion of "Anglicizing" as the policy norm see the treatment of schooling in John Rex and Robert Moore, *Race, Community and Conflict: A Study of Sparkbrook* (London: Oxford University Press, 1967).

45. Department of Education and Science, "The Education of Immigrants," Circular 7/65 to local authorities (1965).
46. Quoted in Deakin, *supra* note 37, at 23.
47. *The Education of Immigrants, supra* note 35, at 119.
48. *Education, supra* note 29, at 28.
49. Quoted in *The West Indian Community, supra* note 29, at 171.
50. Townsend and Brittan, *supra* note 25, *passim.*
51. See generally David Milner, *Children and Race* (London: Penguin, 1975).
52. R. Dhondy, "The Black Explosion in Schools," *Race Today* 44 (February 1974).
53. *The Education of Immigrants, supra* note 35, at 66.
54. Townsend, *supra* note 21, at 60.
55. "Education to counter racial and colour prejudice and promote healthy race relations need not be separated in any way from the normal content of the curriculum" (*The Education of Immigrants, supra* note 35, at 12). See also Raymond Giles, *The West Indian Experience in British Schools* (London: Heineman, 1977).
56. Townsend, *supra* note 21, at 33–34.
57. Little, *supra* note 26, at 81.
58. Liverpool Youth Organization Committee, *Special But Not Separate: A Report on the Situation of Young Coloured People in Liverpool* (Liverpool: 1968); Leonard Bloom, "Study of Bute Town, Cardiff," unpublished paper cited in Nicholas Deakin, *supra* note 37, at 312.
59. Quoted in *Education, supra* note 29, at 21–22.
60. See generally Jones, *supra* note 33, at 180–183.
61. Quoted in Jones, *id.* at 181.
62. Interview with Gordon Renton, Home Office, 5 May 1977.
63. "Funding Multi-Racial Education," *supra* note 39, at 6.
64. *Education, supra* note 29, at 57.
65. Interview with Alan Little, Community Relations Commission, 19 April 1977.
66. Secretary of State for Education and Science, *Educational Disadvantage and the Educational Needs of Immigrants* (London: HMSO, 1974).
67. Interviews carried out by Gail Saliterman with staff mem-

bers at the Centre for Advice and Information on Educational Disadvantage, 21 and 22 April, 1977.
68. *Education, supra* note 29, at 1224–1225.
69. *Secretary of State for Education and Science v. Metropolitan Borough of Tameside*, [1976]3 All ER 665.
70. Michael Locke, *Power and Politics in the School System* 19 (London: Routledge and Kegan Paul, 1974).
71. The Race Relations Act 1976, Section 19, declares that a local authority which discriminates in the provision of educational services is acting "unreasonably," within the meaning of the Education Act 1944, thus authorizing DES intervention.
72. *Tenth Report from the Expenditure Committee, Policy Making in the Department of Education and Science* 110 (London: HMSO, 1976).
73. Kogan, *supra* note 18, at 238.
74. Organization for Economic Cooperation and Development, *Education Development Strategy of England and Wales* 50 (Paris: OECD, 1975). While few educational bureaucracies can be described as "theoretical, futurological, and revolutionary," the stress on consensualism within DES does distinguish it from other, similar bureaus.
75. *Educational Disadvantages and the Educational Needs of Immigrants, supra* note 66, at 13–14.
76. *Education Development Strategy of England and Wales, supra* note 74, at 30.
77. See generally Jones, *supra* note 33. R. H. Tawney, *Equality* (London: Allen and Unwin, 1964) is the ideological forerunner of this movement.
78. Richard Titmuss, *Commitment to Welfare* 26 (London: Allen and Unwin, 1968). For a critical appraisal of Titmuss's work, see David Reisman, *Richard Titmuss: Welfare and Society* (London: Heineman, 1977).
79. Richard Titmuss, *Social Policy* 38 (London: Allen and Unwin, 1974).
80. *Id.*
81. Robert Pinker, *Social Theory and Social Policy* 107 (London: Heineman, 1971).
82. Richard Titmuss, "Goals of Today's Welfare State," in P. Anderson and R. Blackburn, eds., *Towards Socialism* 354 (London: Fontana, 1965).
83. Titmuss, *supra* note 78, at 113–114.
84. Quoted in Pinker, *supra* note 81, at 192. See also Reisman, *supra* note 78, at 91–98, for other redistributive techniques.

85. *Educational Priority, EPA Problems and Policies* (London: HMSO, 1972); interview with A. H. Halsey, former director of the EPA experiment, 26 June 1977.
86. A. Corbett, "Priority Schools," *New Society* 785–787 (30 May 1968).
87. Titmuss, *supra* note 78, at 182.
88. Throughout the nineteenth century, British scholars developed elaborate theories concerning the intellectual inferiority of nonwhites. See Metcalf, *supra* note 4, who views British racism as having "acquired scientific veneer" from this scholarship. Much of the research on the hereditability of intelligence which purports to demonstrate the genetic inferiority of nonwhites has been carried out in Britain. Britons' more general feelings of superiority toward nonwhites have been noted in Chapter One.
89. Community Relations Commission, "Race and Education, A Review" 11 (unpublished paper, 1976).
90. *Educational Disadvantage and the Educational Needs of Immigrants, supra* note 66, at 2.
91. See Ben Heineman, *The Politics of the Powerless* (London: Oxford University Press, 1972); Michael Hill and Ruth Issacharoff, *Community Action and Race Relations* (London: Oxford University Press, 1971).
92. Select Committee on Race Relations and Immigration, *The Organization of Race Relations Administration* xi (London: HMSO, 1974).
93. A Fabian Society Tract scored the 1965 White Paper, which urged restrictions on immigration, a "major retreat from universalist values. . . . The restrictive policies . . . were bound to make racial equality harder to achieve. But they make social equality harder to achieve too."
94. For example Little, *supra* note 26, observes, at 100: "With the exception of extremes, the social and ethnic mix of the school appears to have little influence on the performance of either the indigenous or the settler population." The absence of significant social class diversity among "naturally" mixed communities, and hence the possibility that mixing middle class whites with poor blacks might have salutory effects, goes undiscussed by Little. More generally, because "policy studies" are typically not undertaken in the British academy, the race-relations research tends to be oriented to theory-testing, not policy-shaping.
95. Titmuss, *supra* note 78, at 114.
96. *New York Times*, A5, col. 1, (7 April, 1977).

97. Home Policy Committee, Labour Party, "Race and Education" 1 (unpublished report, March 1977).
98. Interview with John Lyttle, advisor to Shirley Williams, Secretary of State for DES, 24 June 1977. On the West Indian situation, see also John Ogbu, *Minority Education and Caste: The American System in Cross-Cultural Perspective* (New York: Academic Press, 1978).
99. Titmuss, *supra* note 78, at 114.
100. Heineman, *supra* note 91, at 227.
101. John Lyttle, advisor to Shirley Williams, Secretary of State for DES, provided these figures.
102. Sir Edward Boyle, *Race Relations and Education* 7–8 (Liverpool: Liverpool University Press, 1970).
103. *The West Indian Community: Observations on the Report of the Select Committee on Race Relations and Immigration* (London: HMSO, 1978).
104. *Proposals for Replacing Section II of the Local Government Act 1966: A Consultative Document* (Home Office, 1978).
105. David Smith, *Discrimination* 187 (London: Political and Economic Planning, 1976). Compare the assessment of the Community Relations Commission, "Race and Education," *supra* note 89, at 10: The "non-policy" of DES "has left us with a situation of serious underachievement among many minority group children, high youth unemployment. . . ."

three
Busing and (Liberal) Backlash in Britain

1. The Southall-Ealing history is recounted in Maurice Kogan, "Dispersal in the Ealing LEA School System" (Report to the Race Relations Board, July, 1975). This report, together with interviews with Martyn Grubb, Ealing Community Relations Council, 6 May 1977; Tim Otteranger, Ealing Education Authority, 6 May 1977; Vishnu Sardu, former President, Indian Workers' Association, 11 May 1977, provide the primary basis for assessments of the Ealing history.
2. Interviews with Anthony Lester, barrister for the Race Relations Board, 15 April 1977; Geoffrey Bindman, solicitor for the Race Relations Board, 3 May 1977; Sir

Geoffrey Wilson, Chairman of the Race Relations Board, 10 May 1977; Usha Prasha, former officer of the Race Relations Board, 6 June 1977; materials provided by Mary Hunt, staff member, Commission on Racial Equality; and authorized access to unpublished documents on file with the Race Relations Board, provide the primary bases for assessment of the role of the board and the successor commission in the dispersal controversy.

3. Statistics concerning the numbers and concentration of minority students are drawn from the Department of Education's annual publication, *Statistics of Education* (London: HMSO) for the years 1967 through 1973, and from H. E. R. Townsend, *Immigrants in England: The LEA Response* (Slough: National Foundation for Educational Research, 1971).
4. Not that all whites were quiescent; in 1963, white parents of children attending the Lady Margaret School, to which nonwhites were bused, protested the presence of "unclean" Indian students.
5. See generally Anthony Lester and Geoffrey Bindman, *Race and Law in Great Britain* (Cambridge, Mass.: Harvard University Press, 1971). For a discussion of the American situation, see David Kirp and Mark Yudof, *Educational Policy and the Law* (Berkeley: McCutchan, 1974); David Kirp, "Law, Politics, and Equal Educational Opportunity: The Limits of Judicial Involvement," 47 *Harvard Educational Review* 117 (1977).
6. *Secretary of State for Department of Education and Science v. Metropolitan Borough of Tameside* [1976] 3 All E.R. 665 (discussed in Chapter Two).
7. Robert Somers, *The Southern States Since the War, 1870–71*, quoted in Christine Bolt, *Victorian Attitudes to Race* (London: Routledge and Kegan Paul, 1971).
8. Select Committee on Race Relations and Immigration 2 *Education* 19 (London: HMSO, 1973).
9. The quote is attributed to Minister of Education, later Secretary of State for DES, Edward Boyle, in Ealing International Friendship Council, "The Education of the Immigrant Child in the London Borough of Ealing" (unpublished paper, 1969).
10. See Gordon Bowker, *The Education of Coloured Immigrants* (London: Longmans, 1969) for a more extensive discussion of West Bromwich specifically, and the effects of rapid minority student population increases generally.

11. The early history of the Sikh community in Southall is recounted in G. S. Aurora, *The New Frontiersman* (Bombay: Popola Prakashar, 1967).
12. Hansard, vol. 685, cols. 433–444, November 27, 1963 (emphasis added).
13. A circular may embody a DES requirement or recommendation. It is the rough equivalent of an American administrative agency regulation.
14. Department of Education and Science, *The Education of Immigrants*, Circular 7/65 to Local Authorities (June 1965).
15. *Second Report by the Commonwealth Immigrants Advisory Council* (Cmnd. 2266) (London: HMSO, 1964).
16. See Michael Locke, *Power and Politics in the School System* (London: Routledge and Kegan Paul, 1974); Maurice Kogan, *The Politics of Education* (Harmondsworth: Penguin, 1971).
17. Richard Titmuss raises analogous objections to means tests. There are, he asserts, no formulae by which to identify the needy. See Richard Titmuss, *Commitment to Welfare* 119 (London: Allen and Unwin, 1969). On the difficulties of racial identification, see Michael Banton, *Race Relations* (New York: Basic Books, 1967).
18. *Children and Their Primary School: A Report of the Central Advisory Council for Education* (London: HMSO, 1967).
19. *Educational Priority: EPA Problems and Policies* (London: HMSO, 1972).
20. National Association of Schoolmasters, *Education and the Immigrants* (London: NAS, 1969).
21. Select Committee on Race Relations and Immigration, *Education* (London: HMSO, 1973).
22. The Bristol history is recounted in testimony before the Select Committee, *Id.* at 42.
23. For this reason, estimates concerning dispersal consistently underestimate the extent of the practice. Although Townsend, *supra* note 3, states that only 4,000 nonwhite children were dispersed throughout Britain, this is plainly wrong; just two of the dispersing authorities, Ealing and Bradford, dispersed that many nonwhite students.
24. The discussion of London is drawn from interviews with Martin Shipman of the Research Division of ILEA, 20 April 1977, and Roy Truman, ILEA Inspector, 22 April 1977.
25. Quoted in Nicholas Deakin, *Colour, Citizenship and British Society* (London: Panther, 1970).
26. Select Committee, *supra* note 21, at 396.

27. Bernard Coard, *How the West Indian Child Is Made Educationally Sub-Normal in the British School System* 35 (London: New Beacon, 1971).
28. Quoted in Sheila Patterson, *Immigration and Race Relations in Britain, 1960–67* 258 (London: Oxford University Press, 1969).
29. James Coleman et al., *Equality of Educational Opportunity Survey* (Washington: Government Printing Office, 1966).
30. Christopher Jencks, et al., *Inequality* (New York: Basic Books, 1973).
31. Alan Little, "The Performance of Children from Ethnic Minority Backgrounds," 1 *Oxford Review of Education* 129 (1975).
32. See Nancy St. John, *School Desegregation: Outcomes for Children* (New York: John Wiley, 1975).
33. Select Committee on Race Relations and Immigration, *The Problem of Coloured School Leavers* (London: HMSO, 1969).
34. Select Committee, *supra* note 21, vol. 2, *Evidence*, at 175 (hereafter *Evidence*).
35. *Id.* at 177.
36. Department of Education and Science, Education Survey 13, *The Education of Immigrants* (London: HMSO, 1971).
37. For their part, the agencies—the Race Relations Board and, especially, the Community Relations Commission—were supposed to work through existing government agencies, rather than attempting to chart policy on their own.
38. Compare the DES position stated at the Select Committee's 1973 hearings, *Evidence*, *supra* note 34, at 116: "Educationally . . . dispersal has not got the arguments in favour of it now that it had four years ago."
39. Select Committee, *supra* note 21, at 41–43.
40. *Evidence*, *supra* note 34, at 16.
41. *Id.* at 645.
42. *Id.* at 18.
43. Community Relations Commission, *Funding Multi-Racial Education: A National Strategy* 11 (London: CRC, 1976).
44. Kogan, *supra* note 1, at 13, 14, 25, 22.
45. Michael Hill and Ruth Issacharoff, *Community Action and Race Relations* (London: Oxford University Press, 1971).
46. *Evidence, supra* note 34, at 354.
47. West Middlesex Communist Party, "Stop Busing 3000 Children" (Southall, 1974) (mimeographed pamphlet).
48. These figures were introduced at the 1973 Select Committee Hearings, *supra* note 21.

49. Even after the planned new schools are constructed in Southall, an estimated 1,150 students will still have to be bused under the Ealing plan as compared with 2,900 bused in 1975–76.
50. [1971] 2 All E.R. 881.
51. Anthony Lester and Geoffrey Bindman, *supra* note 5, at 269–271.
52. The board's own solicitor, Geoffrey Bindman, faulted the board on just these grounds. See Bindman, "Law and Racial Discrimination—The New Procedure," 4 *New Community* 284 (1975).
53. See note 2, *supra*, for a discussion of sources.
54. Interview with Anthony Lester, *supra* note 2.
55. It was Bradford's dispersal program that had been singled out by HMO Inspector Burrows, during the 1969 Select Committee hearings. See text at note 35, *supra*.
56. City of Bradford Metropolitan Council, *Education in a Multi-Racial Society: The Report of the Joint Working Party on the Education of Immigrants and Their Children* (1976).
57. Interview with Professor Eric Hawkins, 2 May 1978.
58. *Ealing London Borough Council v. Race Relations Board*, [1972] 1 All E.R. 105.
59. For its part, the board was willing to limit the scope of the case to events beginning in the 1976–77 school year, provided that (a) dispersal policy had not materially changed between the time of the Kogan report and 1976, and (b) earlier statements in the public record concerning dispersal could be introduced as evidence. This proposal was designed to avoid the necessity of reviewing actual instances of dispersal from its inception 13 years earlier.
60. *Race Relations Board v. London Borough of Ealing* [1978] 1 All E.R. 497.
61. None of the new Southall schools are, in fact, nonwhite neighborhood schools; they are being built in a predominantly white section of town a mile or more from the predominantly nonwhite Northcote ward, with no apparent minority opposition.
62. *1965 White Paper on Immigration from the Commonwealth* Cmnd. 2379, p. 18 (London: HMSO, 1965).
63. See note 28, *supra*.
64. *Council Housing Purposes, Procedures, and Priorities* 135, 136 (London: HMSO, 1969). For a thorough discussion of this policy, see David McKay, *Housing and Race in Industrial Society* (London: Croon Helm, 1977).

65. Community Relations Commission, *Housing Choice and Ethnic Concentration* (London: CRC, 1977).
66. Catherine Jones, *Immigration and Social Policy in Britain* 251 (London: Tavistock, 1977).
67. Compare Jones, *Id.* at 241, discussing the reluctance of housing authorities to admit that they maintain racially separate records:

> Most revealing of all, perhaps, was the written questionnaire response of one department where, having described separate records as a useful tool whereby a check could be kept, over time, on the standard of treatment afforded to immigrant clients, this answer was then erased; to be replaced by the simple statement that no records were in fact being kept.

68. See Raymond Giles, *The West Indian Experience in British Schools* (London: Heineman, 1977).
69. Hill and Issacharoff, *supra* note 45, at 51.
70. See David Kirp, "School Desegregation and the Limits of Legalism," 47 *Public Interest* 101 (Spring 1977).

four
Toward an Appraisal of Racial Explicitness

1. H. E. R. Townsend, *Immigrants in England: The LEA Response* 60 (Slough: National Foundation for Educational Research, 1971).
2. Alan Little, "The Performance of Children from Ethnic Minority Backgrounds in Primary Schools," 1 *Oxford Review of Education* 71, 81 (1975).
3. See Sidney Webb, "Grants in Aid: A Criticism and a Proposal (1920)" in Charles Benson, ed., *The Economics of Public Education* 218 (Boston: Houghton Mifflin, 1961), for a discussion of the social benefits of more equal provision of education.
4. Select Committee on Race Relations and Immigration, 1 *Education* 23 (London: HMSO, 1973) (quoting from the statement of the National Association of Schoolmasters).
5. A. H. Halsey, "Towards Meritocracy? The Case of Britain," in Jerome Karabel and A. H. Halsey, eds., *Power and Ideology in Education* 173 (New York: Oxford University Press, 1977).

6. On this point, see Raymond Boudon, *Education: Opportunity and Social Equality* (New York: John Wiley, 1973); Lester Thurow, "Education and Economic Equality," *Public Interest* 66 (Summer 1972).
7. Herman Melville, *Billy Budd* 77 (Indianapolis: Bobbs-Merrill, 1975).
8. Select Committee, *supra* note 4.
9. *New York Times* 69, cols. 6–7 (March 1, 1970).
10. "A Case of 'Benign Neglect,' " *Newsweek* 25, col. 2 (March 16, 1970).
11. *New York Times* 69, col. 2 (March 1, 1970).
12. "Speech on Moving His Resolutions for Conciliation with the Colonies," March 22, 1775, in 2 *The Words of Edmund Burke* 117–118 (Boston: Little Brown, 1865): "Through a wise and salutory neglect, a generous nature has been suffered to take her own way to perfection." Albert Camus makes quite different use of a similar phrase at the end of *The Stranger*. Meursault, condemned to death, comes to accept "the benign indifference of the universe" (*The Stranger* 154 [New York: Vintage, 1946]).
13. For a journalistic recounting of the National Front's history, see Martin Walker, *The National Front* (London: Fontana, 1977).
14. *Washington Post* A-7, col. 1 (February 6, 1978). See also A. Howard, "Maggie's Scapegoat," *New Republic* 20 (May 13, 1978). Since Thatcher's immigration-limiting suggestions would have almost no effect on the number of nonwhites in Britain (the total nonwhite population would be an estimated 3.2 million, rather than the projected 3.3 million), the thrust of Thatcher's effort is symbolic, an attempt to turn nonwhites into scapegoats for Britain's assorted ills.
15. The West Indians are primarily concentrated in southeast England, where two-thirds of that population lives, and secondarily in the West Midlands. The Asians are predominantly to be found in the Southeast, West Midlands, and to a lesser extent in Yorkshire and Humberside. Within these regions, they are concentrated in particular enumeration districts (units of about 450): half of the immigrants live in enumeration districts 10 percent or more nonwhite, which account for just 5 percent of Britain's population. See David Smith, *Racial Disadvantage in Britain* 36–39 (Harmondsworth: Penguin, 1977).
16. Interview with A. Sivanandan, 15 April 1977.
17. See D. Moynihan, "The Schism in Black America," *Public Interest* 3 (Spring 1972).

18. Alan Marsh, "Who Hates the Blacks?" *New Society* 649 (September 23, 1976).
19. This discussion is drawn from Community Relations Commission, *Some of My Best Friends . . . A Report on Race Relations Attitudes* (1976).
20. Alan Little and David Kohler, "Do We Hate Blacks?" *New Society* 184 (January 27, 1977).
21. See Smith, *supra* note 15, at 127–151.
22. *Id.* at 285–291.
23. *Id.* at 105–126. The letters did not explicitly state the applicants' race, but provided information—concerning, for example, country of origin—that would enable an employer to draw the intended inference.
24. W. W. Daniel, *Racial Discrimination in England* 76 (Harmondsworth: Penguin, 1968).
25. Smith, *supra* note 15, at 285–291.
26. That fewer nonwhites have personally experienced discrimination does not necessarily mean that white behavior has changed. It might be the case that nonwhites who have suffered (or heard of others who suffered) discrimination do not put themselves in situations where they would undergo such an experience. At the least, this may be one explanation for the concentration of nonwhites in particular neighborhoods and particular places of employment.
27. Smith, *supra* note 15, at 104.
28. *Id.* at 230–242.
29. Edmund Burke, quoted in Irving Kristol, "Decentralization for What?" *Public Interest* 17 (Spring 1968).
30. 735 H. C. Deb. col. 1252, 8 Nov. 1966 (Norman St. John Stevas, M.P., in a debate over antidiscrimination legislation).
31. Philippe Nonet and Philip Selznick, *Law and Society in Transition: Toward Responsive Law* 37 (New York: Harper Colophon, 1978). This argument is couched in general terms, without specific reference to Britain.
32. U.S. Dept. of Health, Education, and Welfare, Office of Civil Rights, Data Branch, *Directory of Public Elementary and Secondary Schools in Selected Districts, Fall 1970* (Washington, D.C.: Government Printing Office).
33. U.S. Bureau of the Census, 1 *Census of the Population* 1 (Washington, D.C.: Government Printing Office, 1970). The "minority" population here includes persons of Spanish origin or descent. If those are excluded, as is the practice of the Census Bureau, the percentage black rises to 88.7.
34. See generally Lawrence Levine, *Black Culture and Black*

Consciousness: Afro-American Folk Through From Slavery to Freedom. (New York: Oxford University Press, 1977).
35. See pages 10–13 *supra,* which treats this issue.
36. *Green v. County School Board, New Kent County,* 391 U.S. 430, 438 (1968).
37. See Bernard Schwartz and Harold Wade, *Legal Control of Government* (Oxford: Clarendon Press, 1972).
38. This discussion is largely borrowed from my essay "School Desegregation and the Limits of Legalism," 47 *Public Interest* 101 (Spring 1977).
39. *Bradley v. Milliken,* 418, U.S. 717, 764 (1974). (White J., dissenting) (emphasis in original).
40. *Dayton Board of Education v. Brinkman,* 433 U.S. 406 (1977).
41. *Lau v. Nichols,* 414 U.S. 563 (1974).
42. Comment, "Alternative Schools for Minority Students: The Constitution, the Civil Rights Act, and the Berkeley Experiment," 61 *California Law Review* 858 (1973).
43. See Anthony Lester, "Foundational Rights in the United Kingdom; The Law and the British Constitution," 125 *University of Pennsylvania Law Review* 337 (1976).
44. For a discussion of judicial reticence with respect to racial discrimination, see pages 19–21, *supra.*
45. See generally the treatment of the Department of Education and Science in Chapter Two, *supra.*
46. William Julius Wilson, *The Declining Significance of Race* 1, 2, 153 (Chicago: University of Chicago Press, 1978). See also Richard B. Freeman, *Black Elite: The New Market for Highly Educated Black Americans* (New York: McGraw Hill, 1977); Daniel P. Moynihan, *Coping: On the Practice of Government* (New York: Vintage, 1975).
47. Moynihan, *supra* note 17.
48. See generally Angus Campbell and Howard Schuman, "Racial Attitudes in Fifteen American Cities," Survey Research Center, Institute for Social Research, the University of Michigan, printed in *Supplemental Studies for The National Advisory Commission on Civil Disorders* (New York: Praeger, 1968).
49. The efforts of black political leader Jesse Jackson are aimed at encouraging literacy among black youth. See Thomas Sowell, "Patterns of Black Excellence," 44 *Public Interest* 26 (Spring 1976).
50. A study undertaken by the U.S. Department of Housing and Urban Development found whites favored over blacks in

29.1 percent of rental situations, 21.5 percent of all sales situations. Black and white testers were used, and instances in which blacks were favored were subtracted from the total to produce a "net" discrimination. Office of Policy Development and Research, Department of Housing and Urban Development, "The Fair Housing Evaluation," April 16, 1978.

51. Data contained in this paragraph are taken from Seymour Lipset and William Schneider, "An Emerging National Consensus," *New Republic* 8 (October 15, 1977). With respect to belief in discrimination, blacks' perceptions are very different: in a 1977 Harris survey, only one-third of all whites but three-quarters of all blacks see discrimination as preventing blacks from achieving "full equality."
52. *Swann v. Charlotte-Mecklenburg Board of Education*, 402 U.S. 1 (1971).
53. *Keyes v. School District No. 1, Denver,* 413 U.S. 189 (1973).
54. For a criticism of the Court's position, see Leno Graglia, *Disaster by Decree: The Supreme Court Decision on Race and Schools* (Ithaca: Cornell University Press, 1976); Nathan Glazer, *Affirmative Discrimination* (New York: Basic Books, 1976). For a defense, see Paul Dimond, "School Desegregation in the North: There is But One Constitution." 7 *Harvard Civil Rights-Civil Liberties Law Review* 4 (1973).
55. See John Coons and Stephen Sugarman, *Education by Choice: The Case for Family Control* 109–130 (Berkeley and Los Angeles: University of California Press, 1978).
56. For an assessment of the competing positions, see Allan Sindler, "Equality of Opportunity: Preferential Admission to Law School for Minorities," in Allan Sindler, ed., *America in the Seventies* 354–355. (Boston: Little Brown, 1977); Barry Gross, ed., *Reverse Discrimination* (New York: Prometheus, 1977); Marshall Cohen, Thomas Nagel, and Thomas Scanlon, eds., *Equality and Preferential Treatment* (Princeton: Princeton University Press, 1977).
57. J. R. Pole, *The Pursuit of Equality in American History,* 354–355 (Berkeley and Los Angeles: University of California Press, 1978).
58. *Regents of University of California v. Bakke,* 98 S. Ct. 2733 (1978).
59. See Richard Kluger, *Simple Justice* (New York: Pantheon, 1975).
60. See David McKay, *Housing and Race in Industrial Society* (London: Croon Helm, 1977).

61. For a discussion of dispersal in Ealing, see Chapter Three, *supra*.
62. See David Kirp, "Advice to DES: Get Off the Fence," *Times Educational Supplement* 2 (July 1, 1977).
63. See generally Orlando Patterson, *Ethnic Chauvinism: The Reactionary Impulse* (New York: Stein and Day, 1977); Nathan Glazer and Daniel P. Moynihan, eds., *Ethnicity* (Cambridge, Mass.: Harvard University Press, 1975).
64. Philip Mason, *Prospero's Magic* 123–124 (London: Oxford University Press, 1964).
65. Compare Steven Marcus, "Their Brothers' Keepers," in Willard Gaylin, Ira Glasser, Steven Marcus, and David Rothman, *Doing Good: The Limits of Benevolence* (New York: Pantheon, 1978).

Index

Designer: Wolfgang Lederer
Compositor: Viking Typographics
Printer: Thomson-Shore
Binder: Thomson-Shore
Text: VIP Century
Display: VIP Helvetica
Cloth: Joanna Arrestox B11000
Paper: 50lb P&S offset vellum B32